This Journal
Belongs To:

_____

© 2019 Crystal Gator - All Rights Reserved

Mandalas of Love Journal & Coloring Book

Artist Decean Ioan of Pixaroma
Provided by license to Crystal Gator

Follow us for new release announcements:

Instagram
CrystalGatorWA

Twitter
CrystalGator

Facebook
@CrystalGator

No part of this book may be reproduced or transmitted in any form or by any means, electronic or mechanical, including photocopying, recording, or by any information storage or retrieval system, without written permission from the publisher.

The information provided within this book is for general information purposes only. While we try to keep the information up-to-date and correct, there are no representations or warranties, express or implied, given about the completeness, accuracy, reliability, suitably, or availability with respect to the information, products, services, or related graphics contained in this book for any purpose.

© 2019 by Crystal Gator - All rights reserved.

Have a question or concern? Contact us.
Crystal Gator | Staff@CrystalGator.com

Important Dates

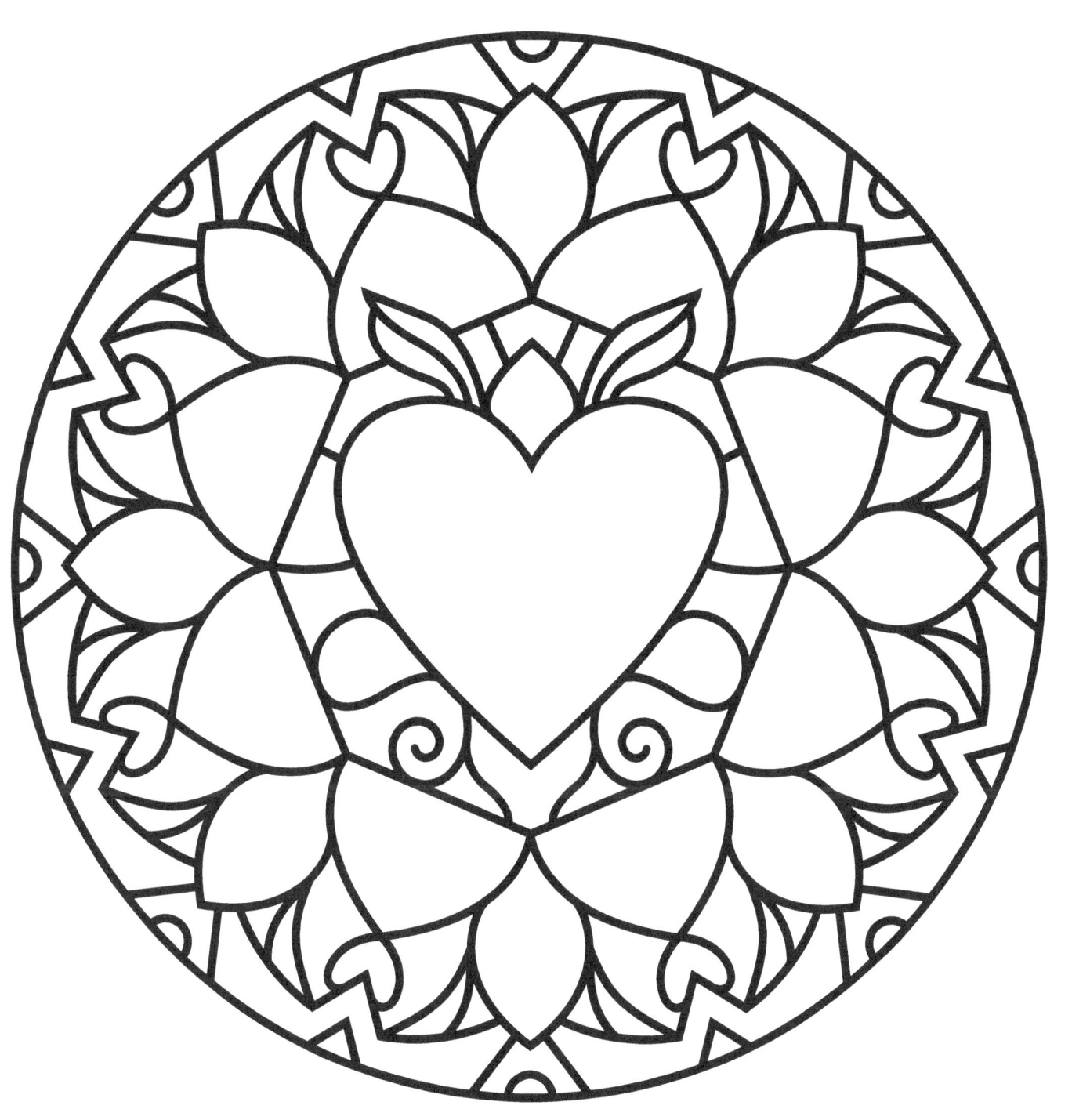

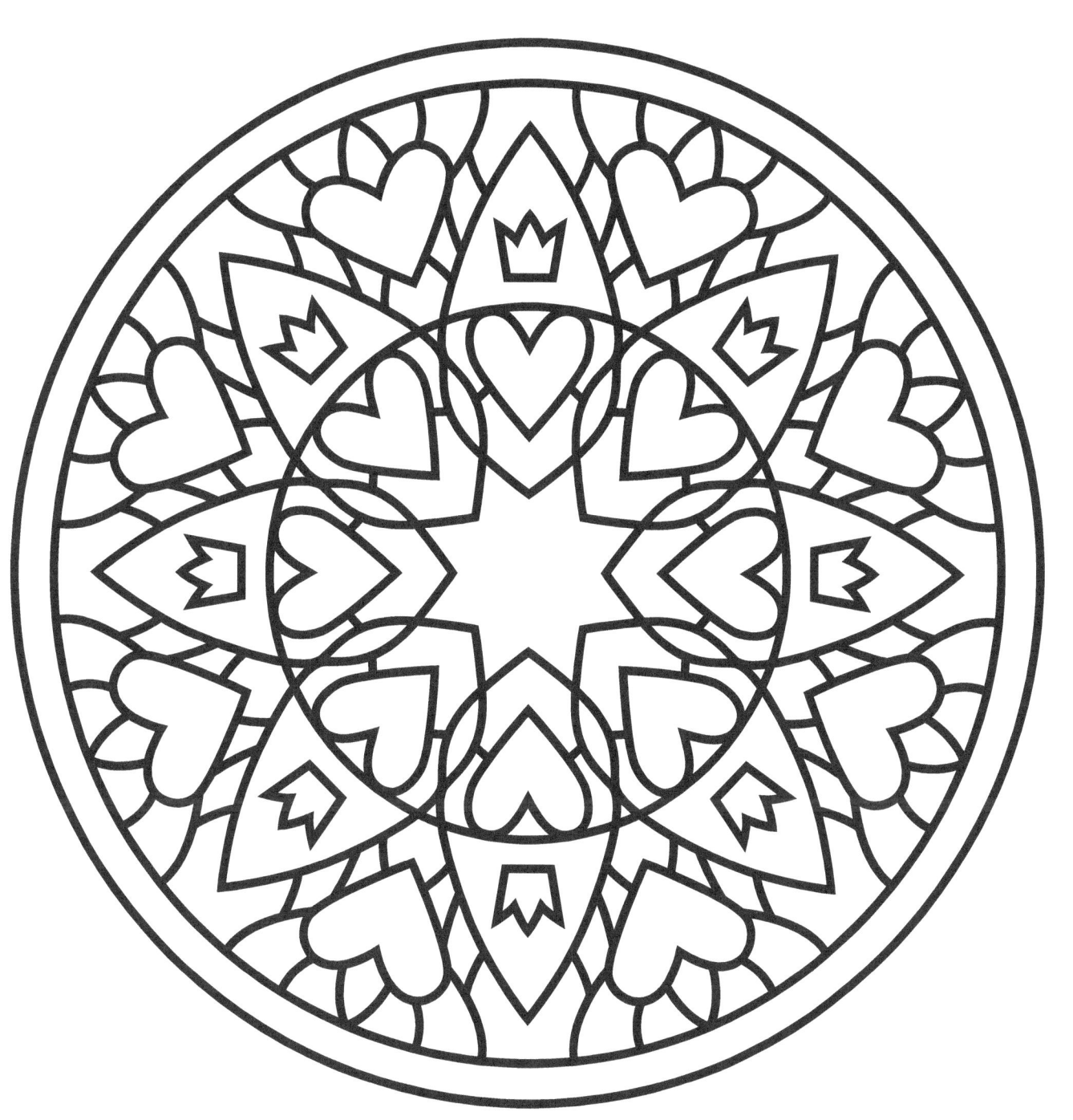

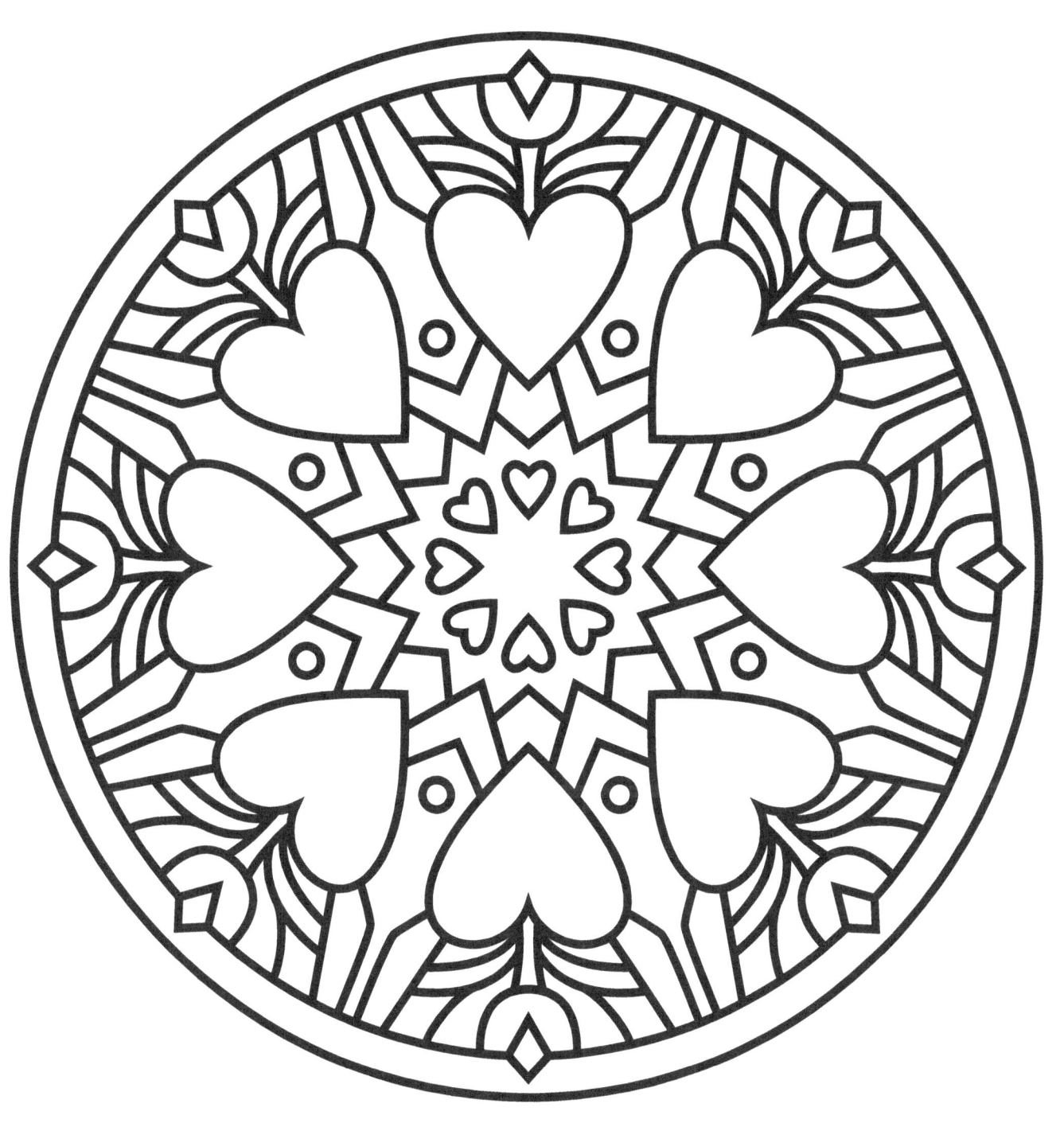

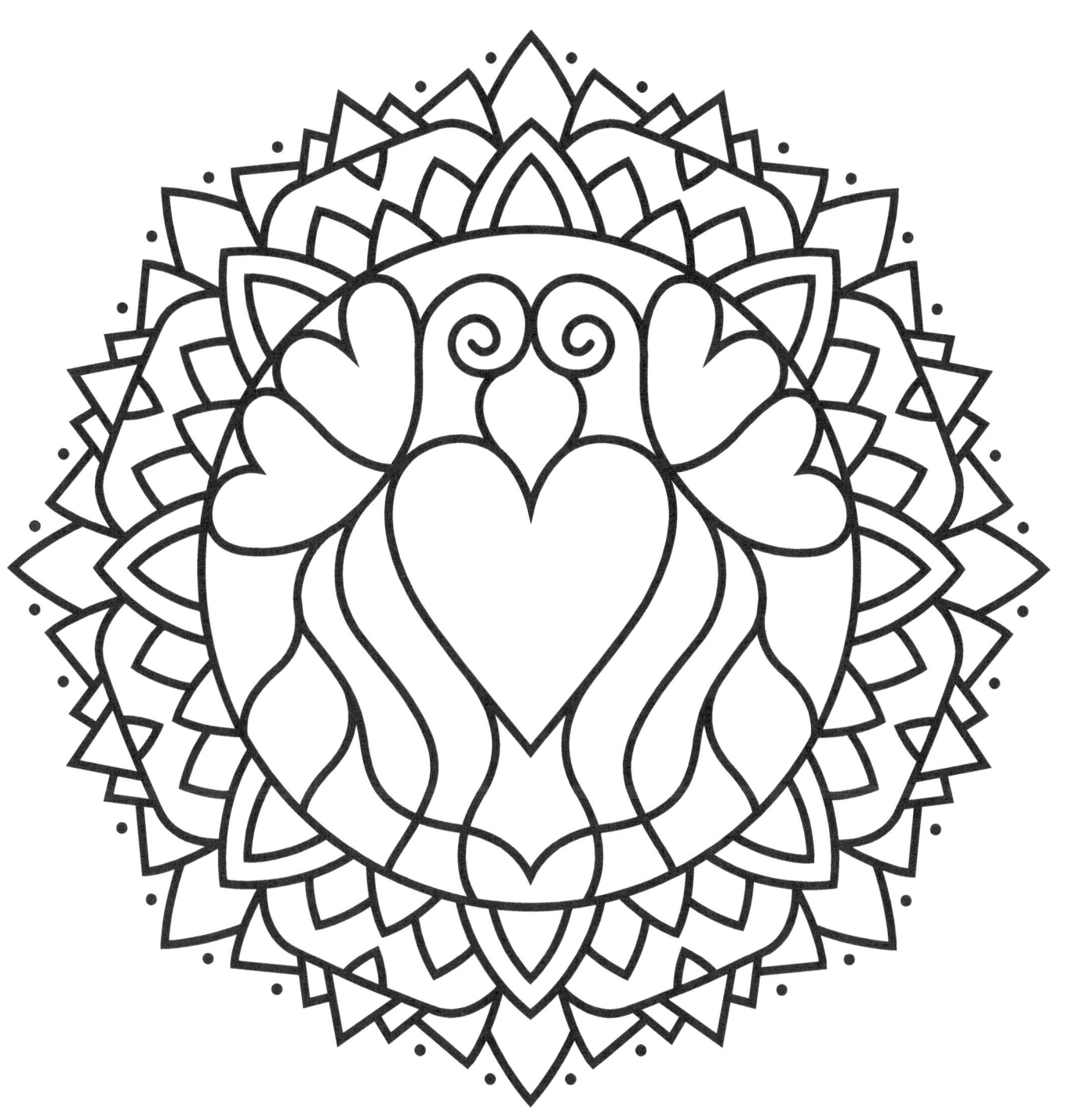

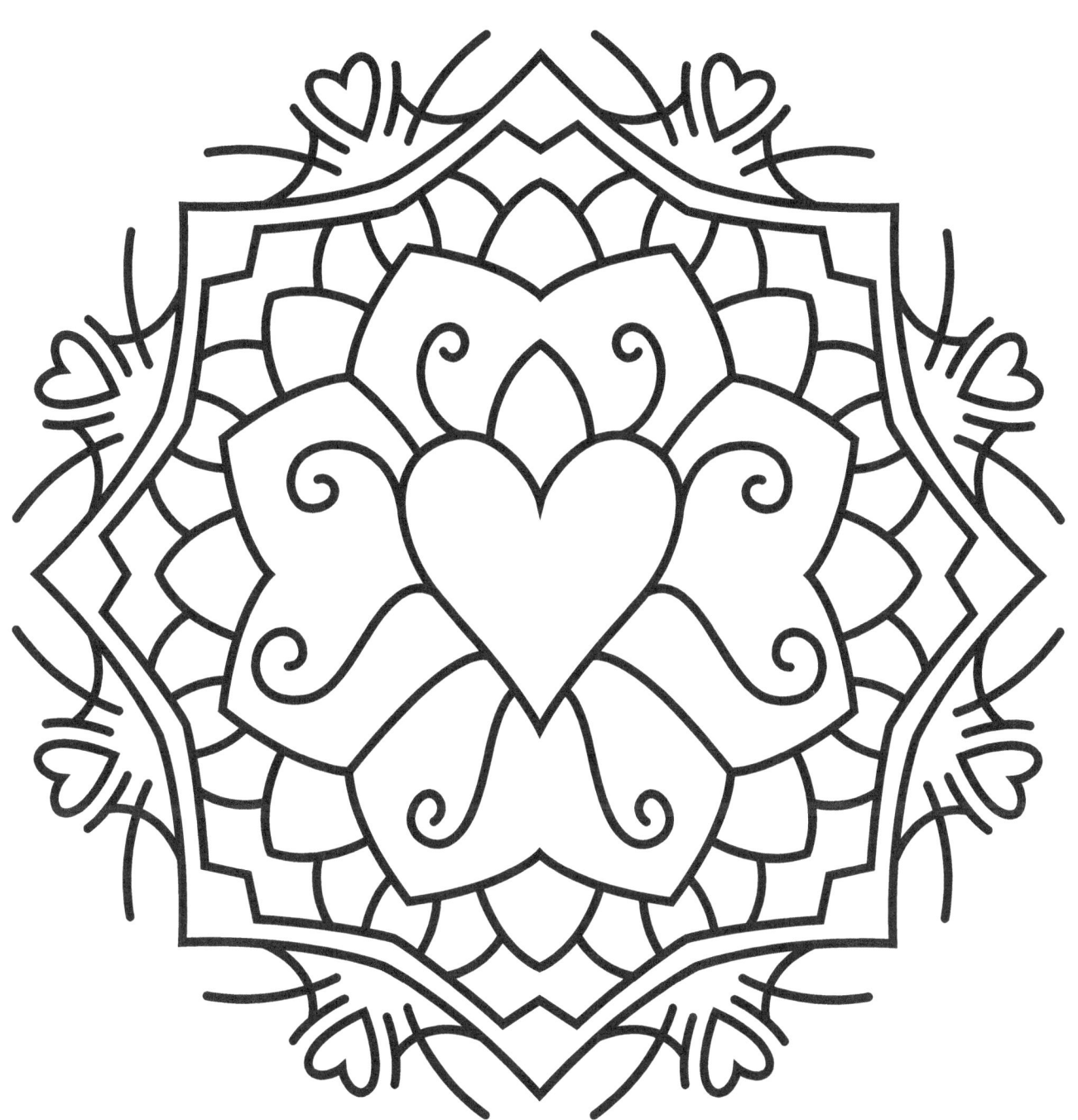

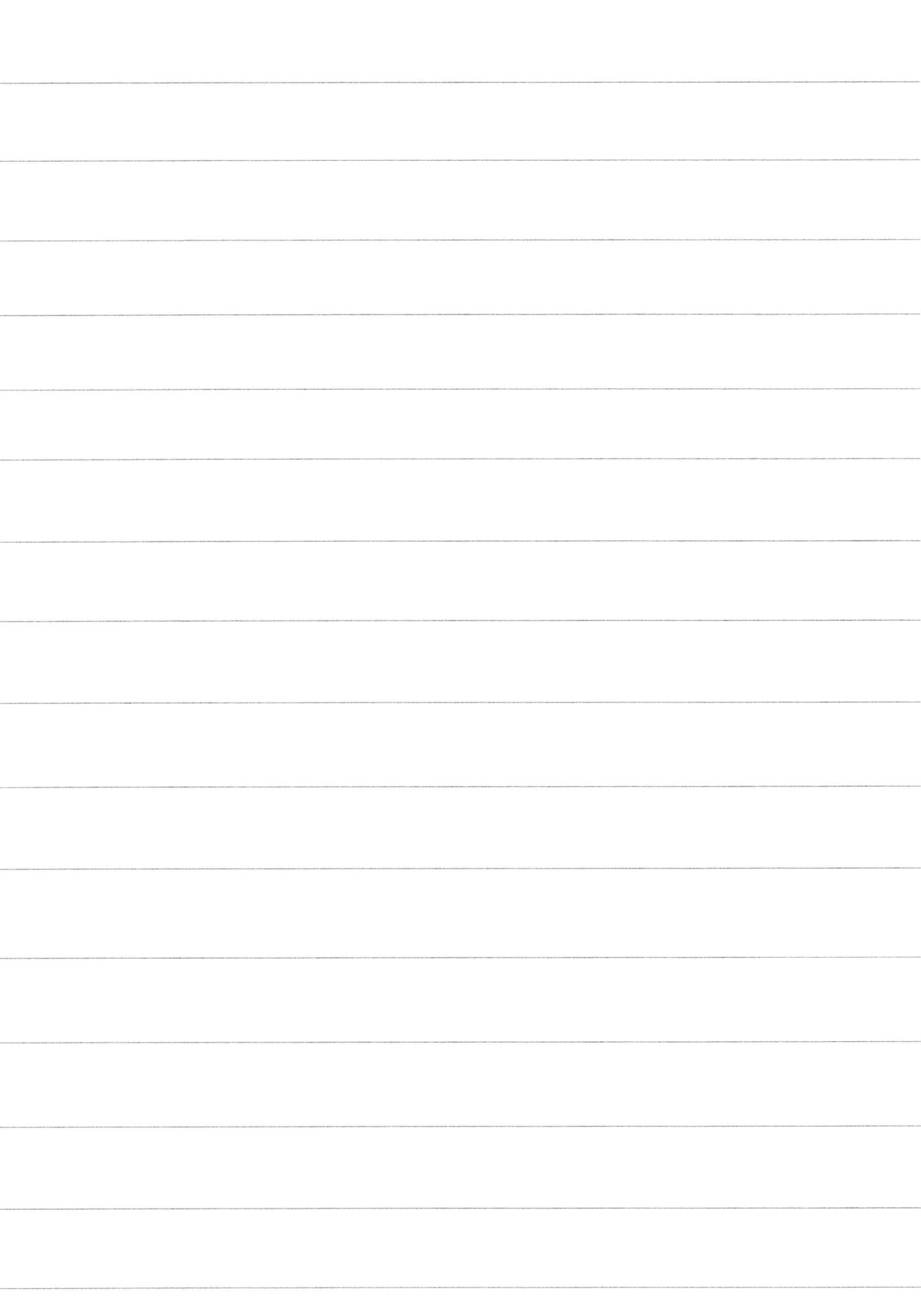

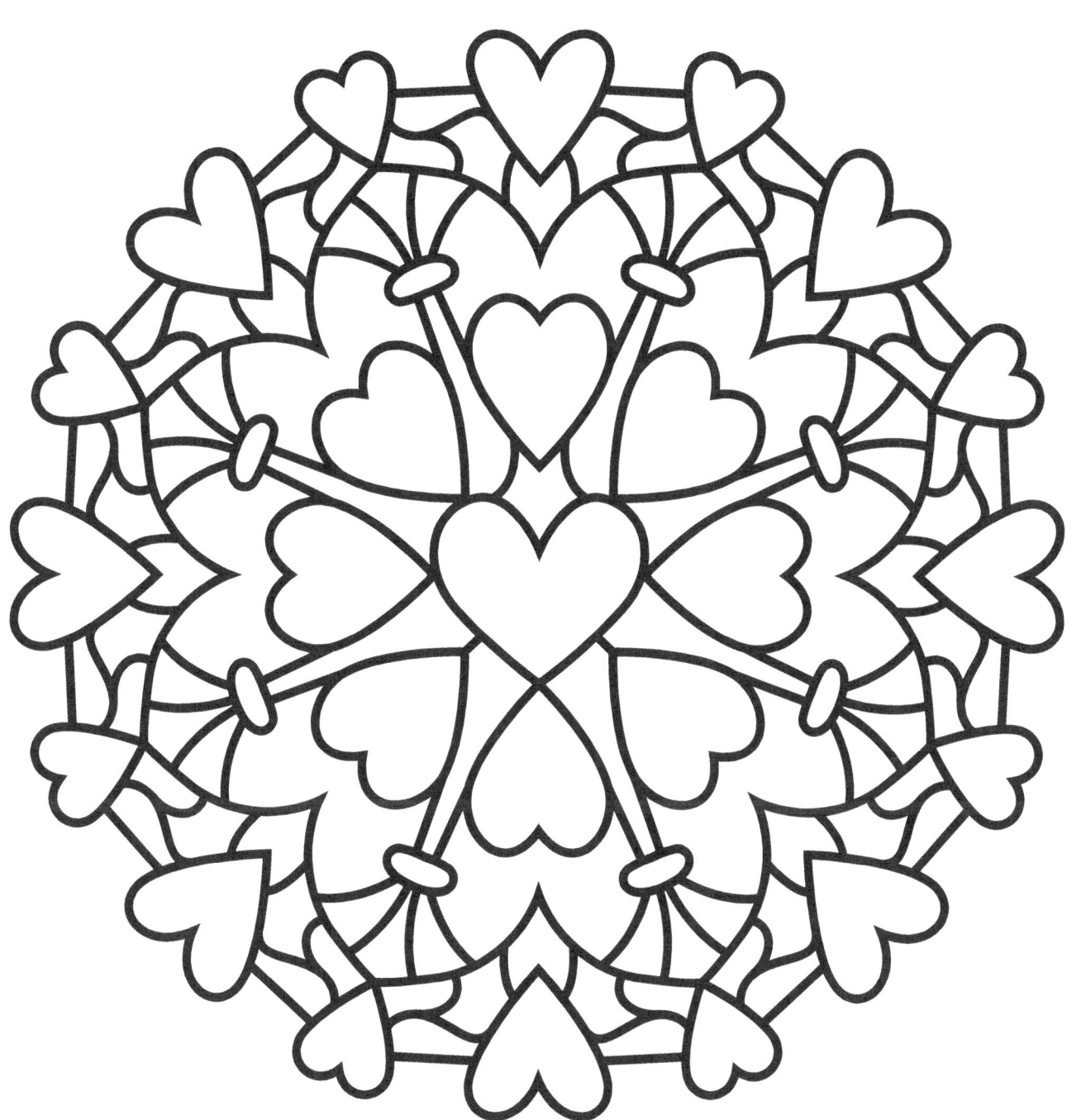

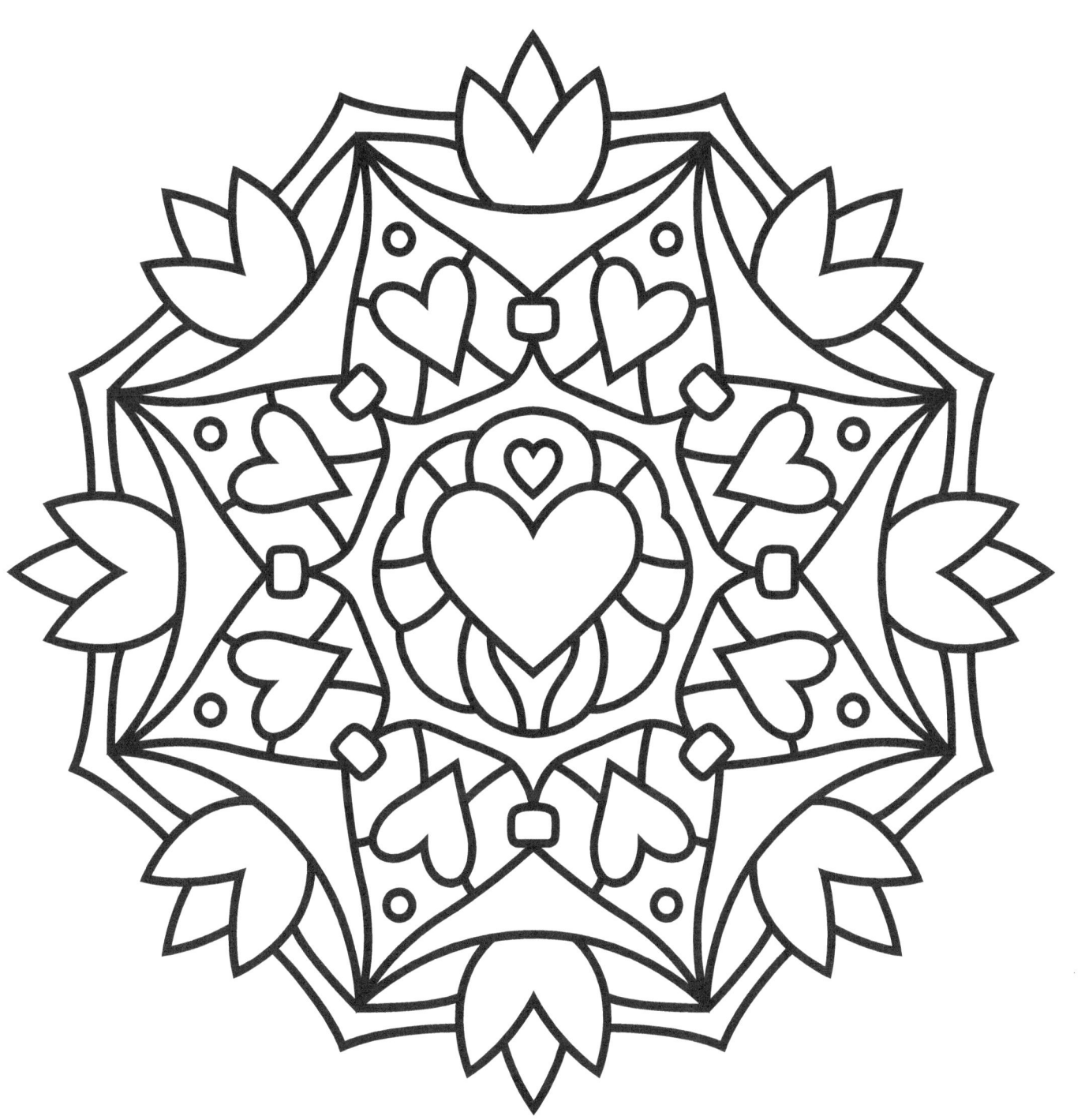

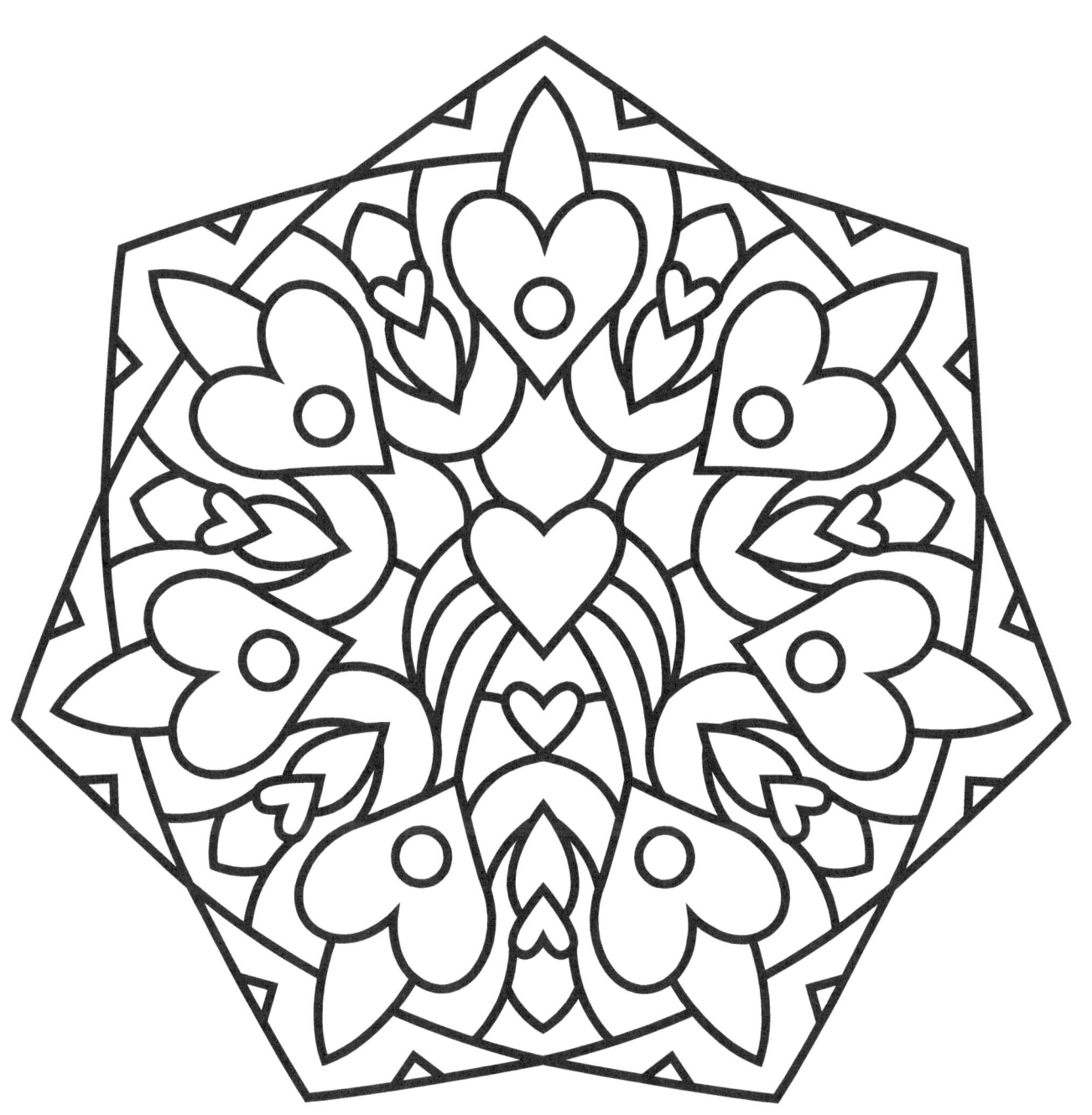

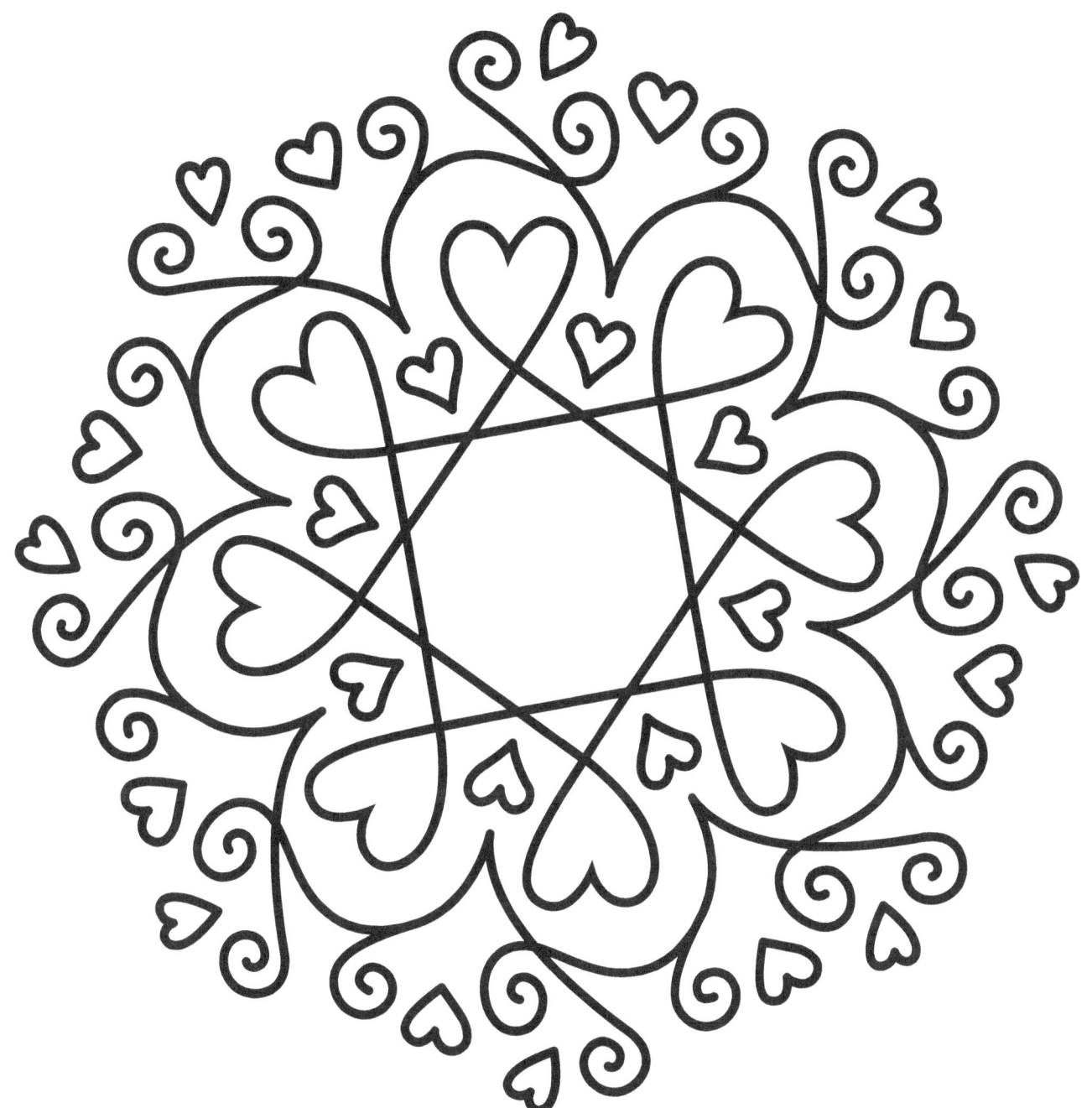

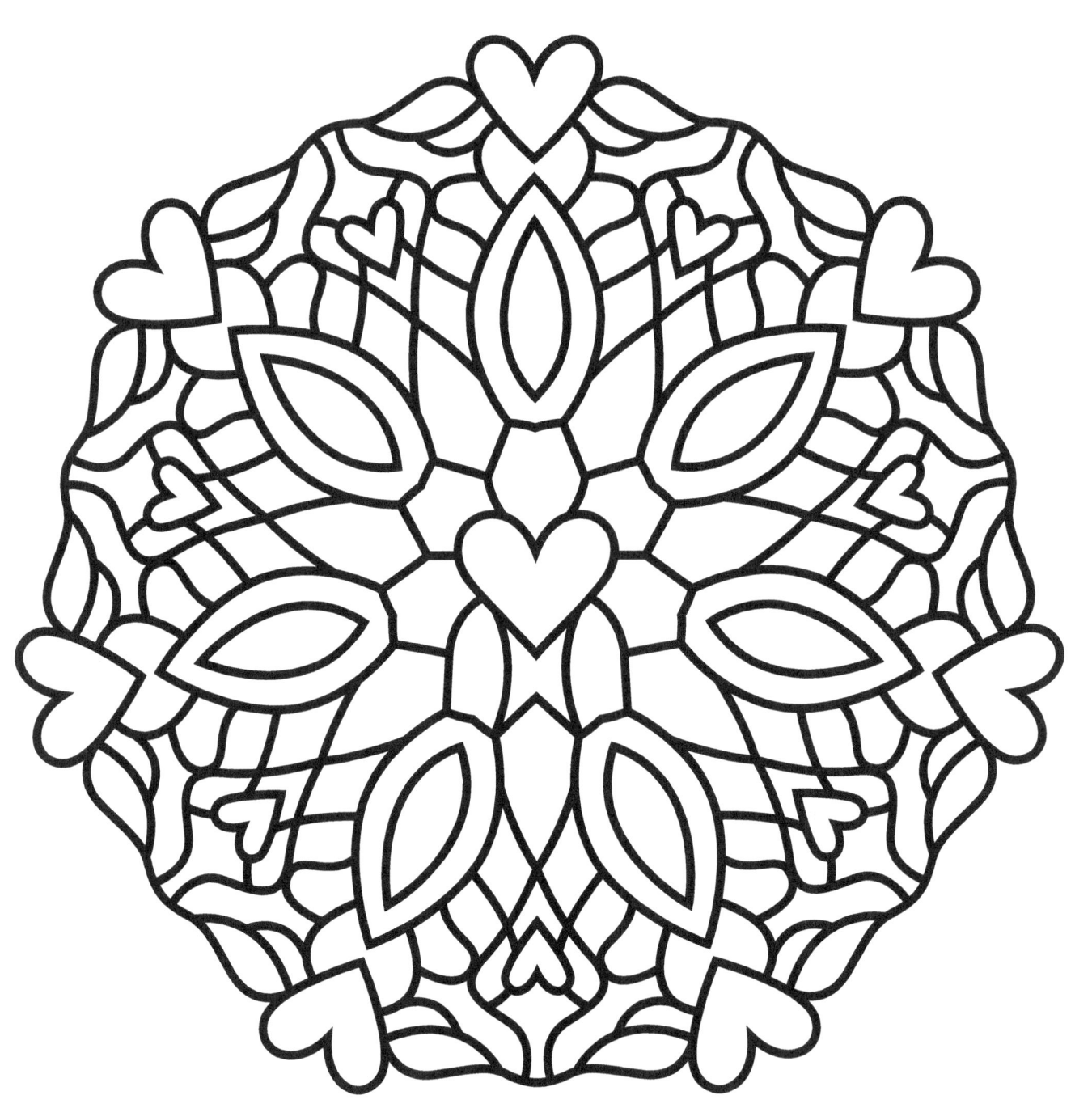

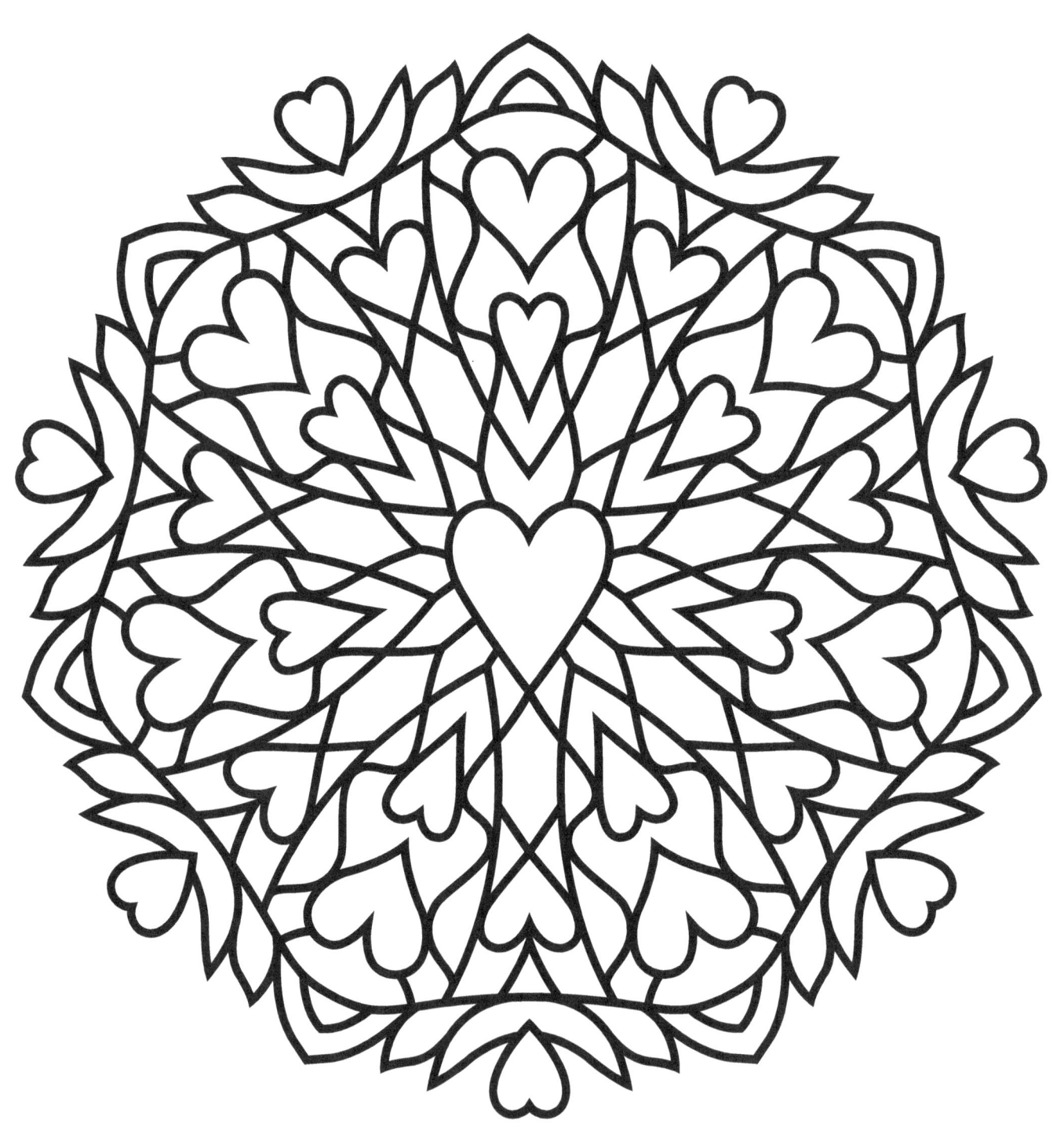

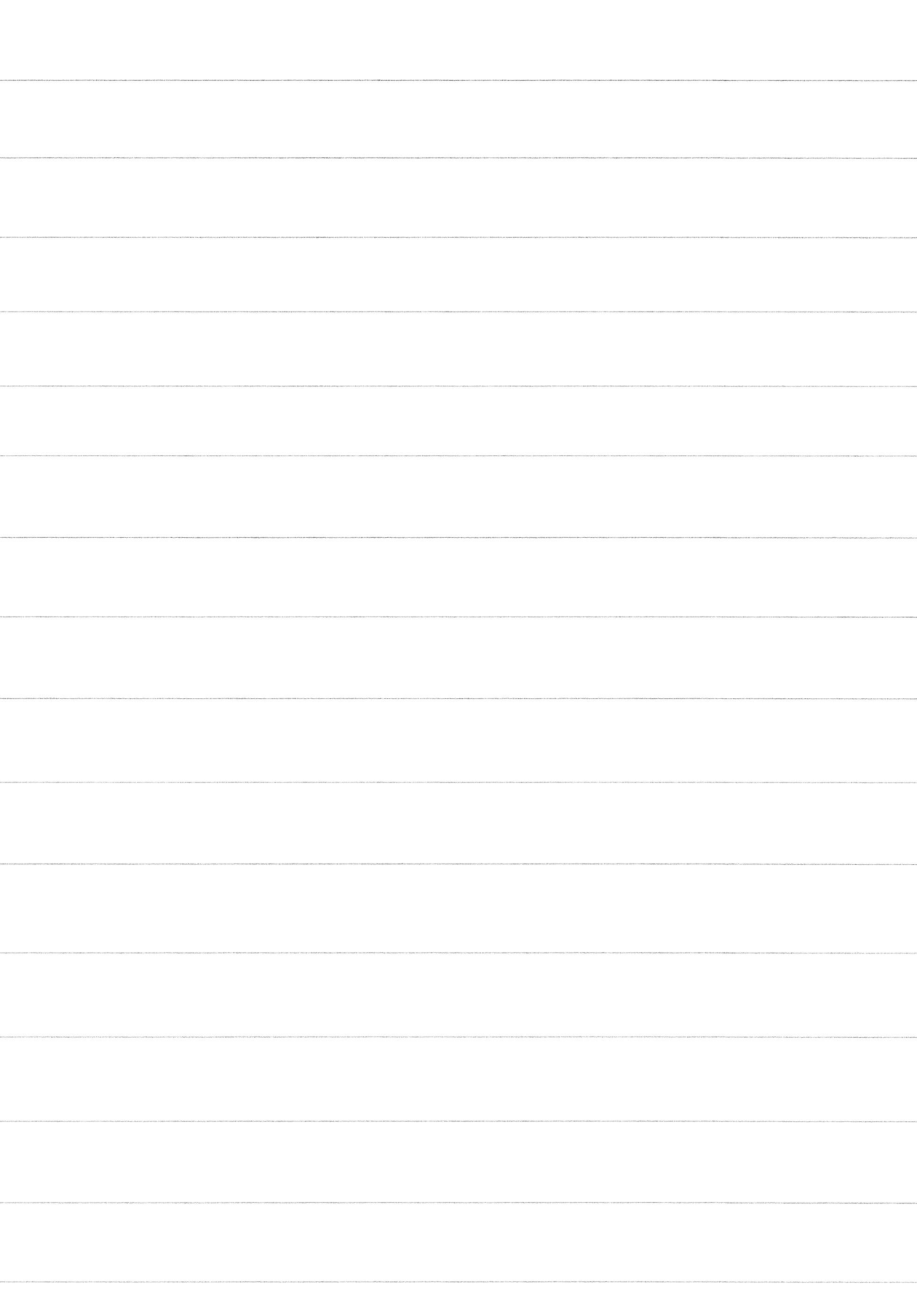

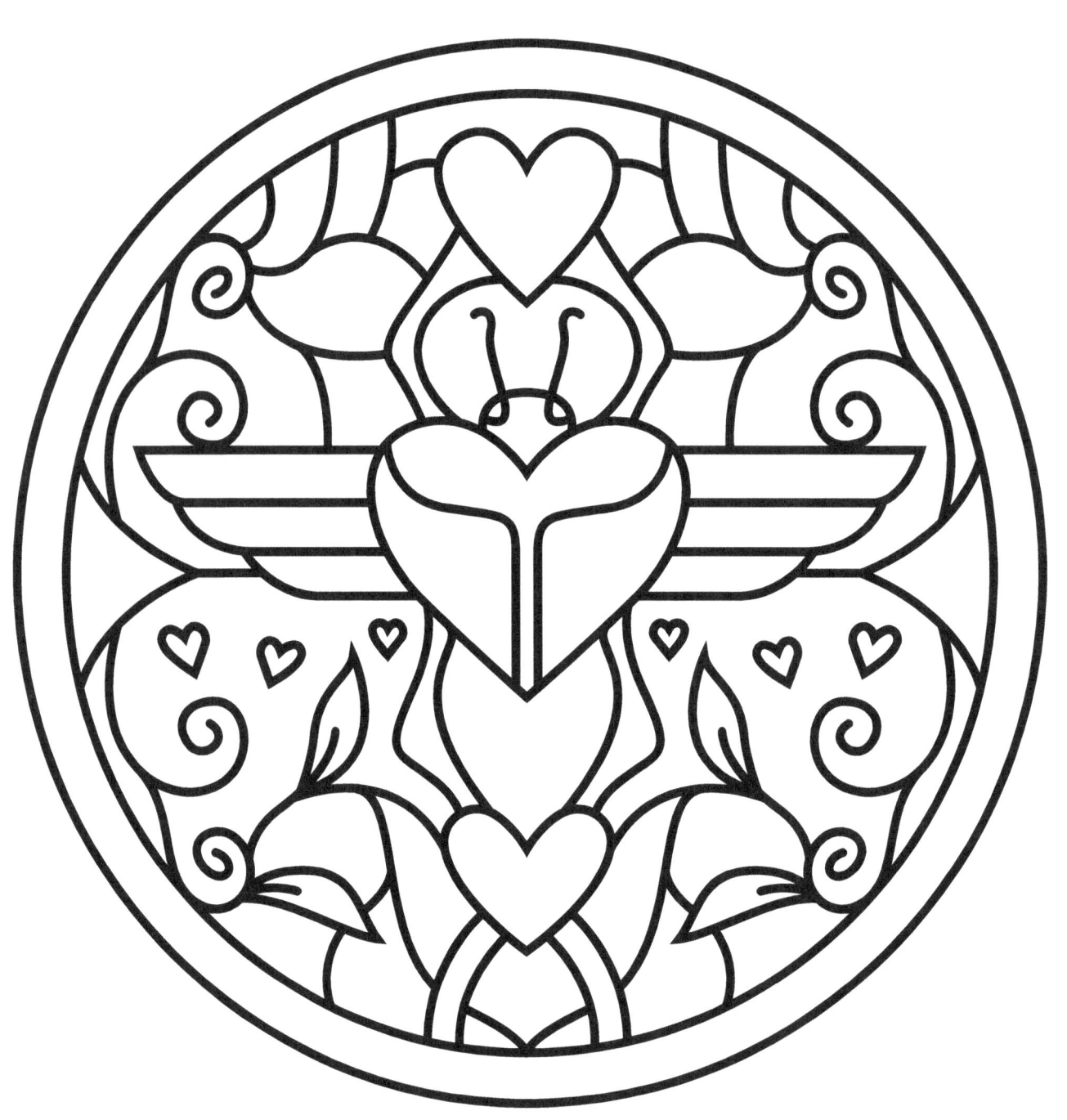

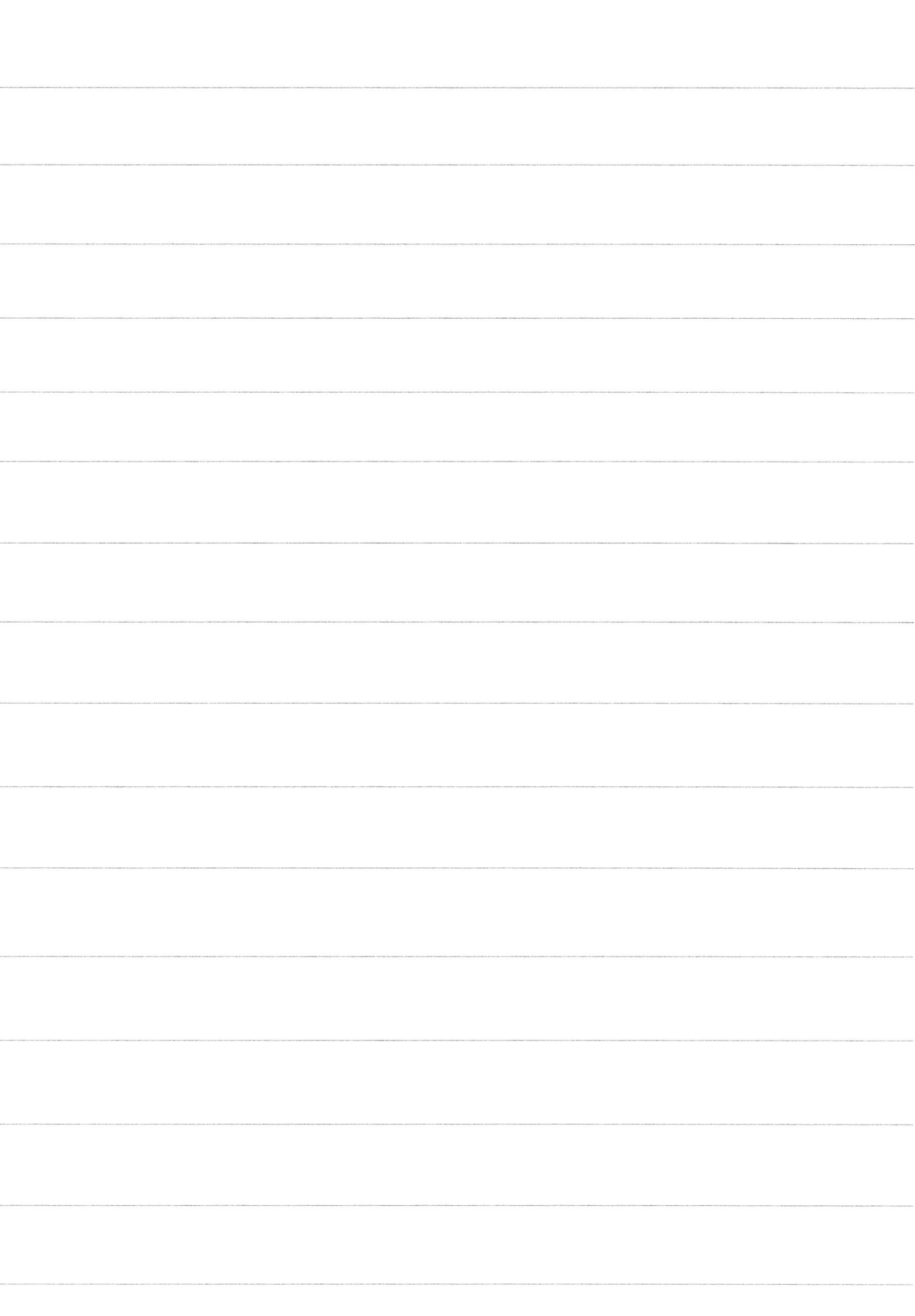

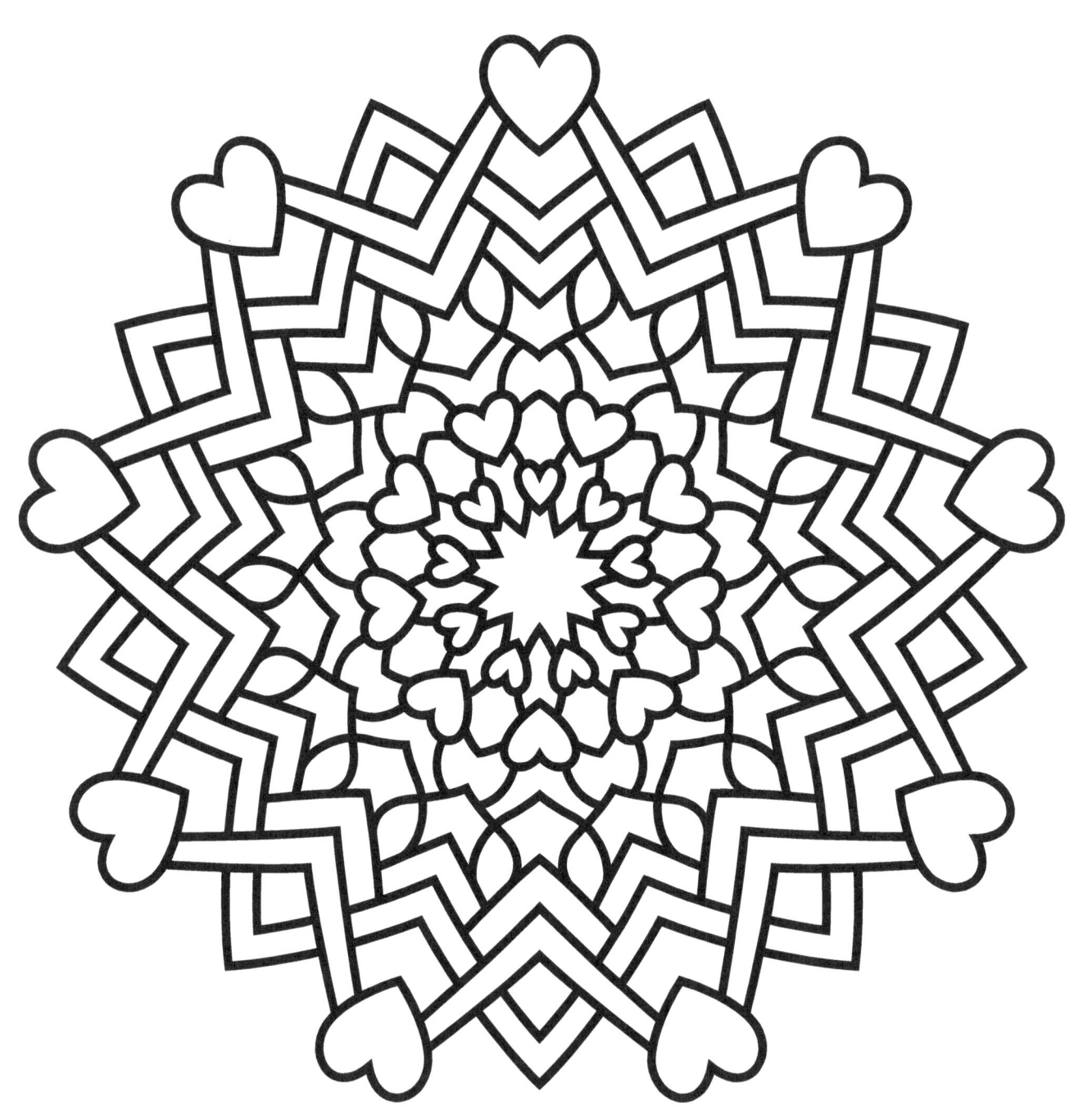

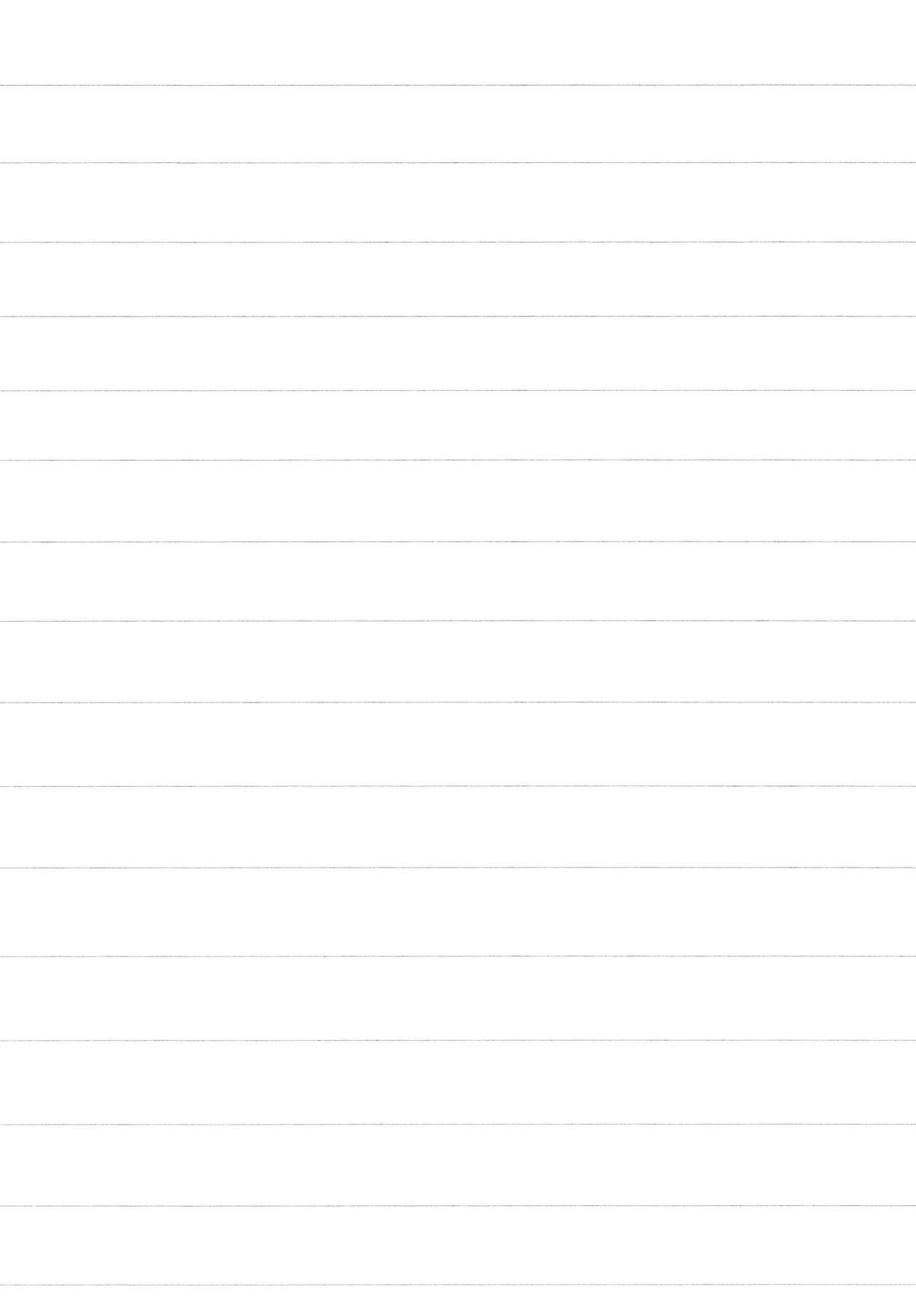

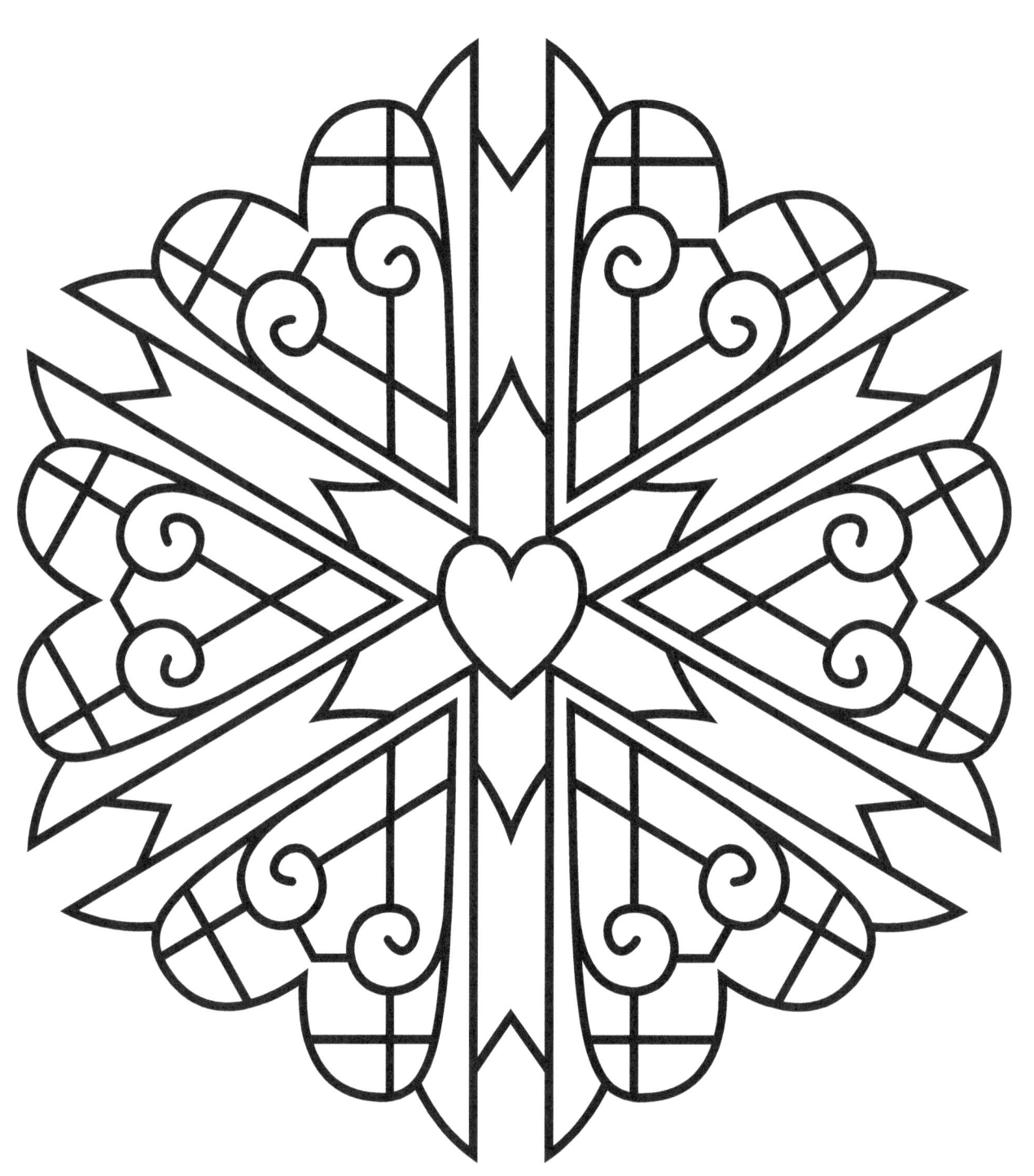

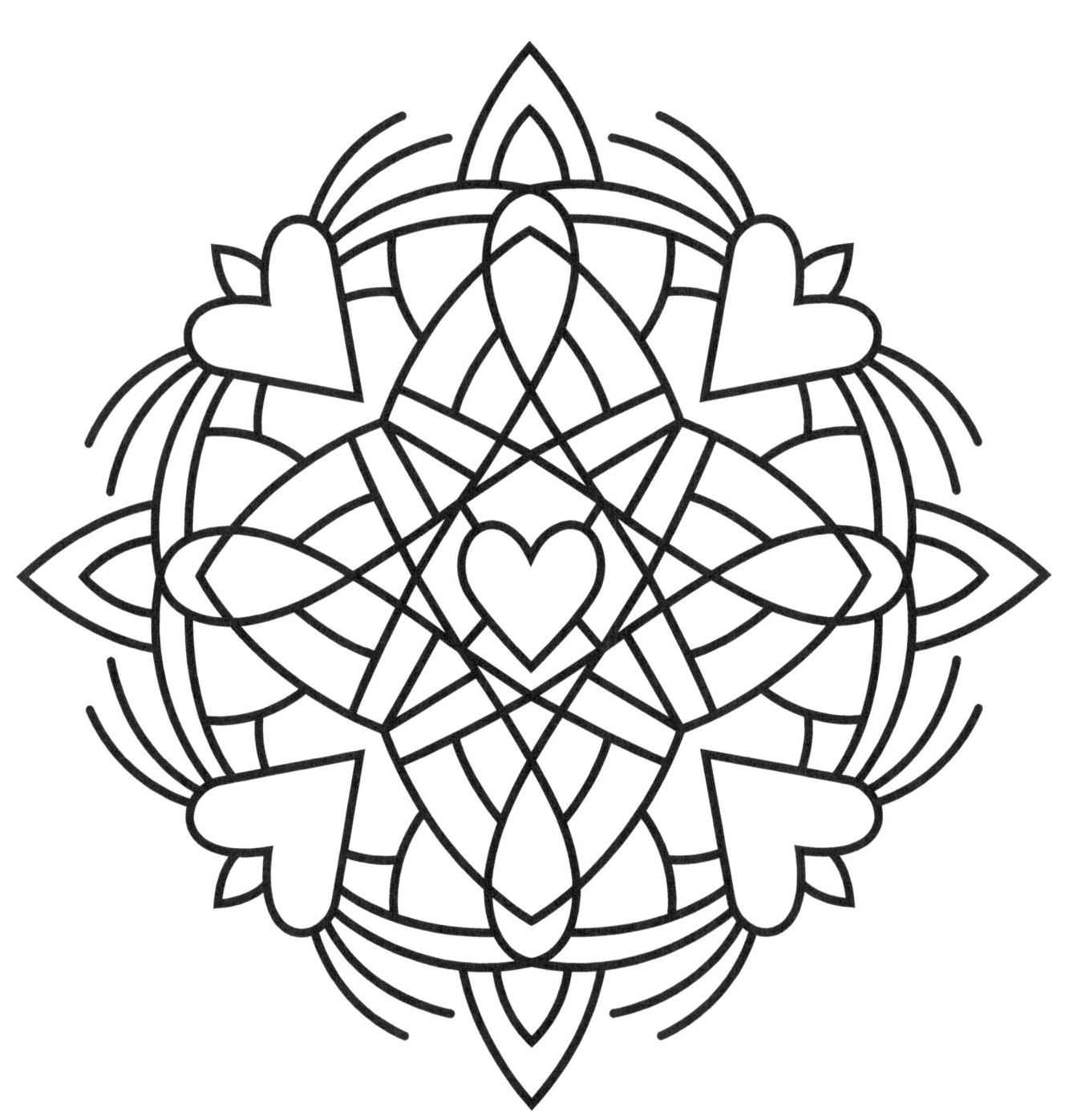

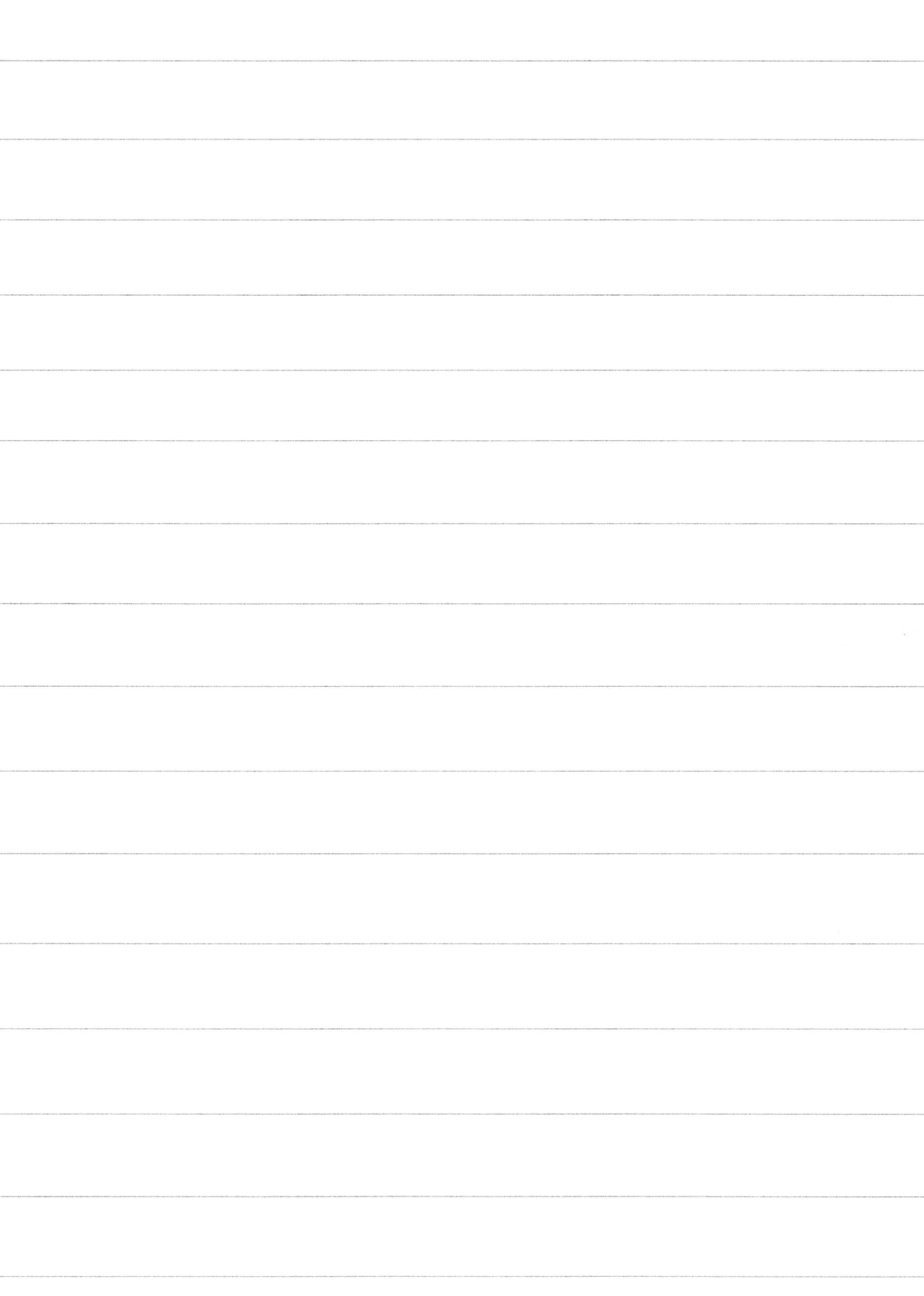

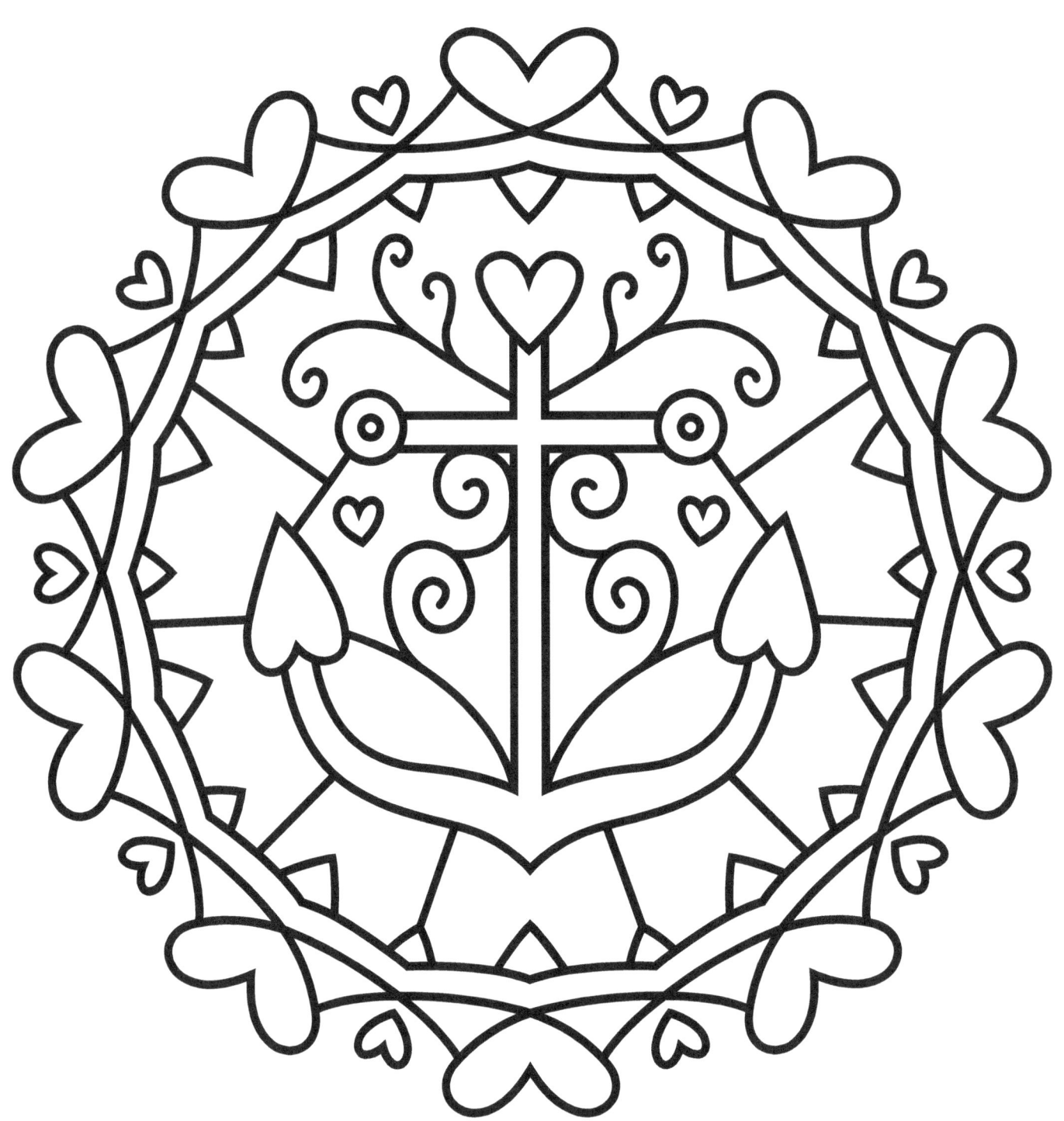

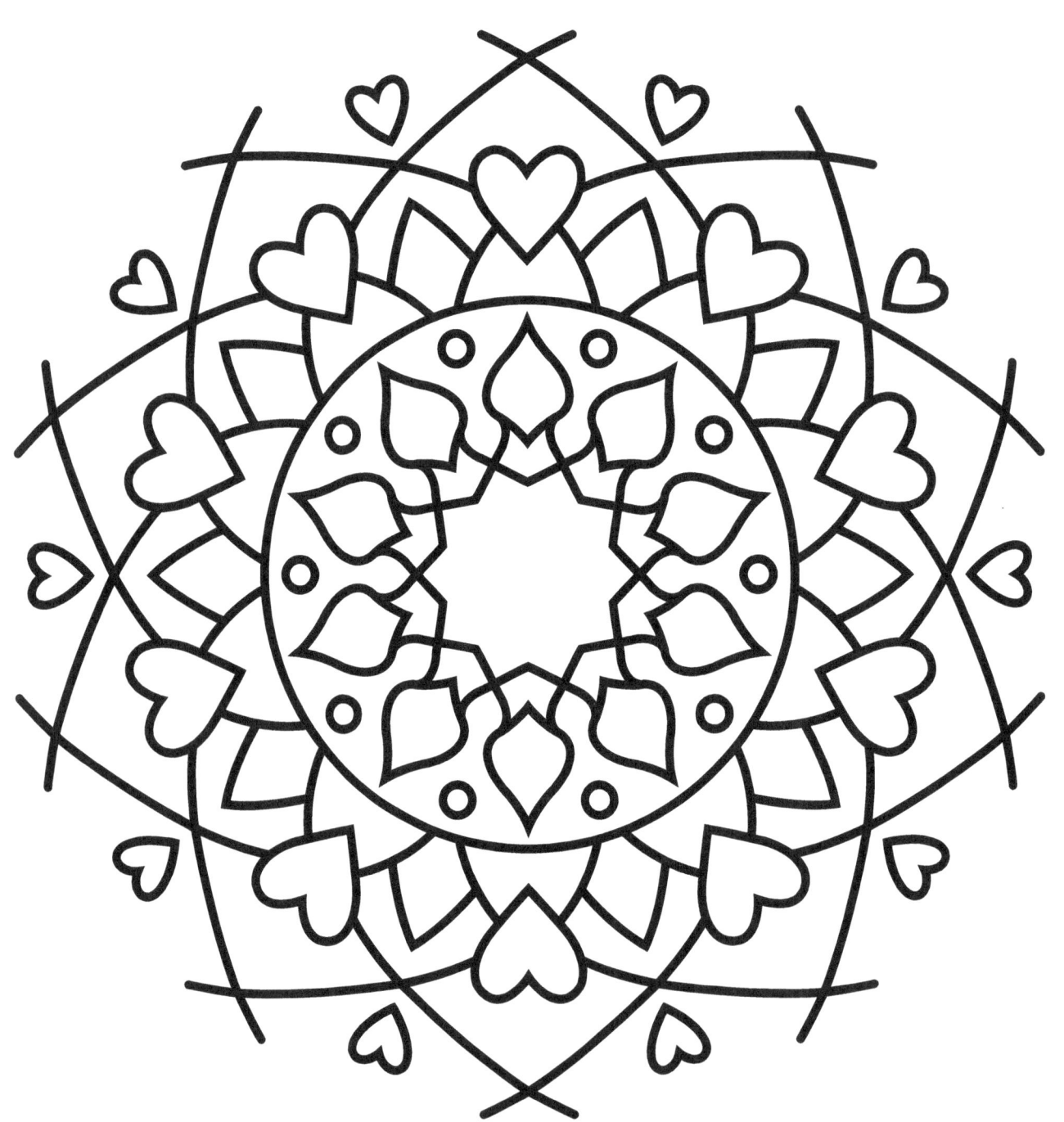

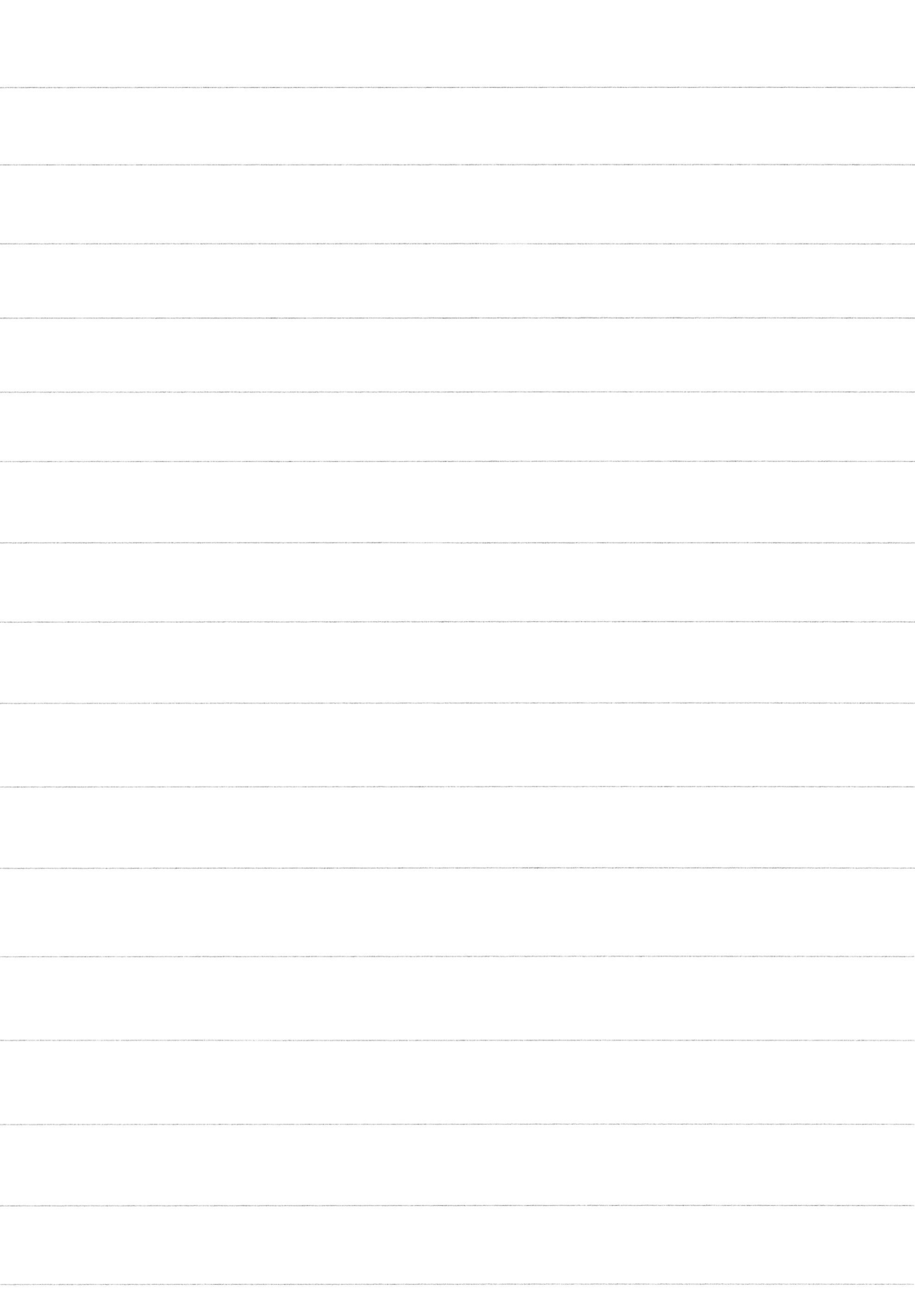

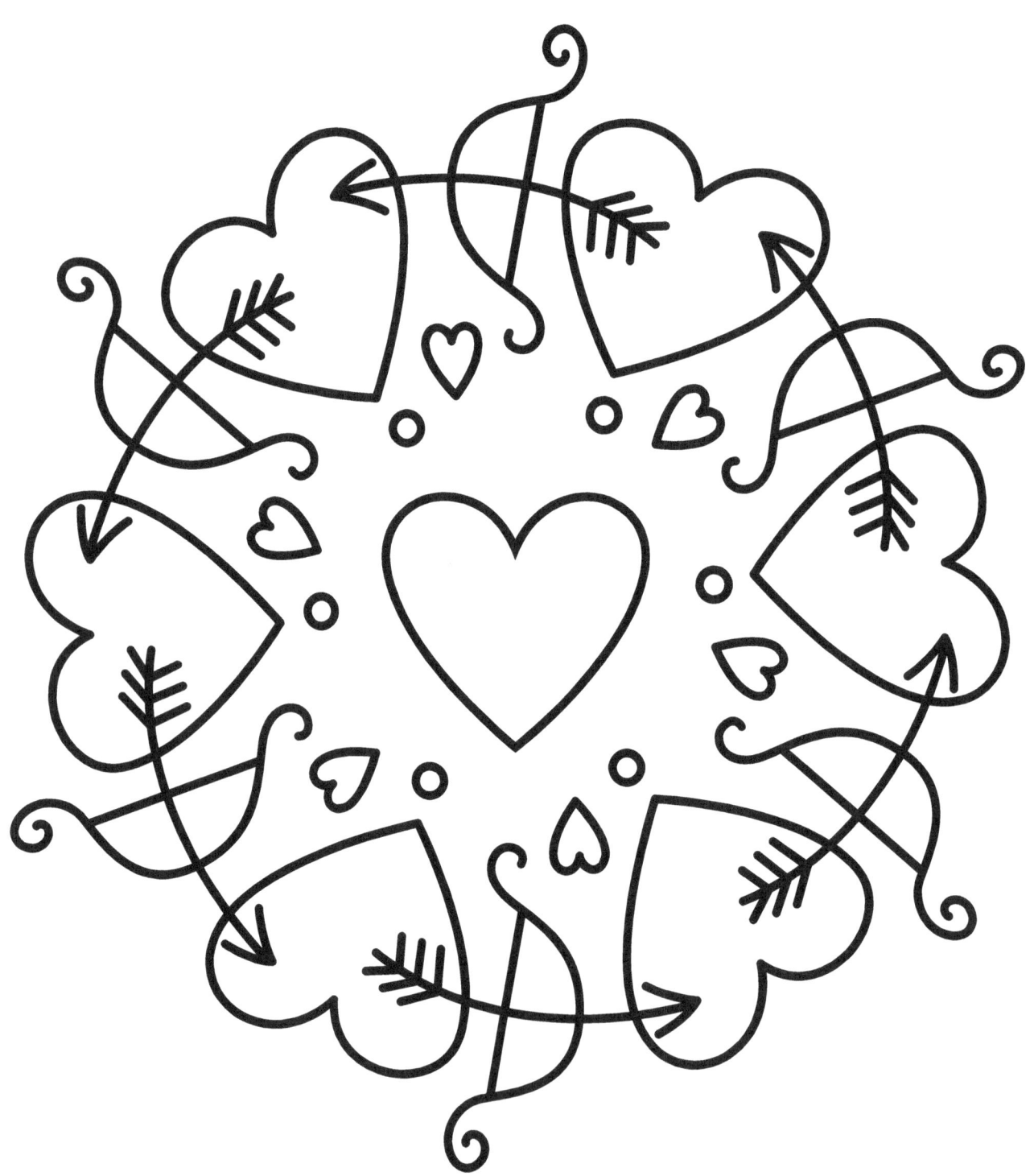

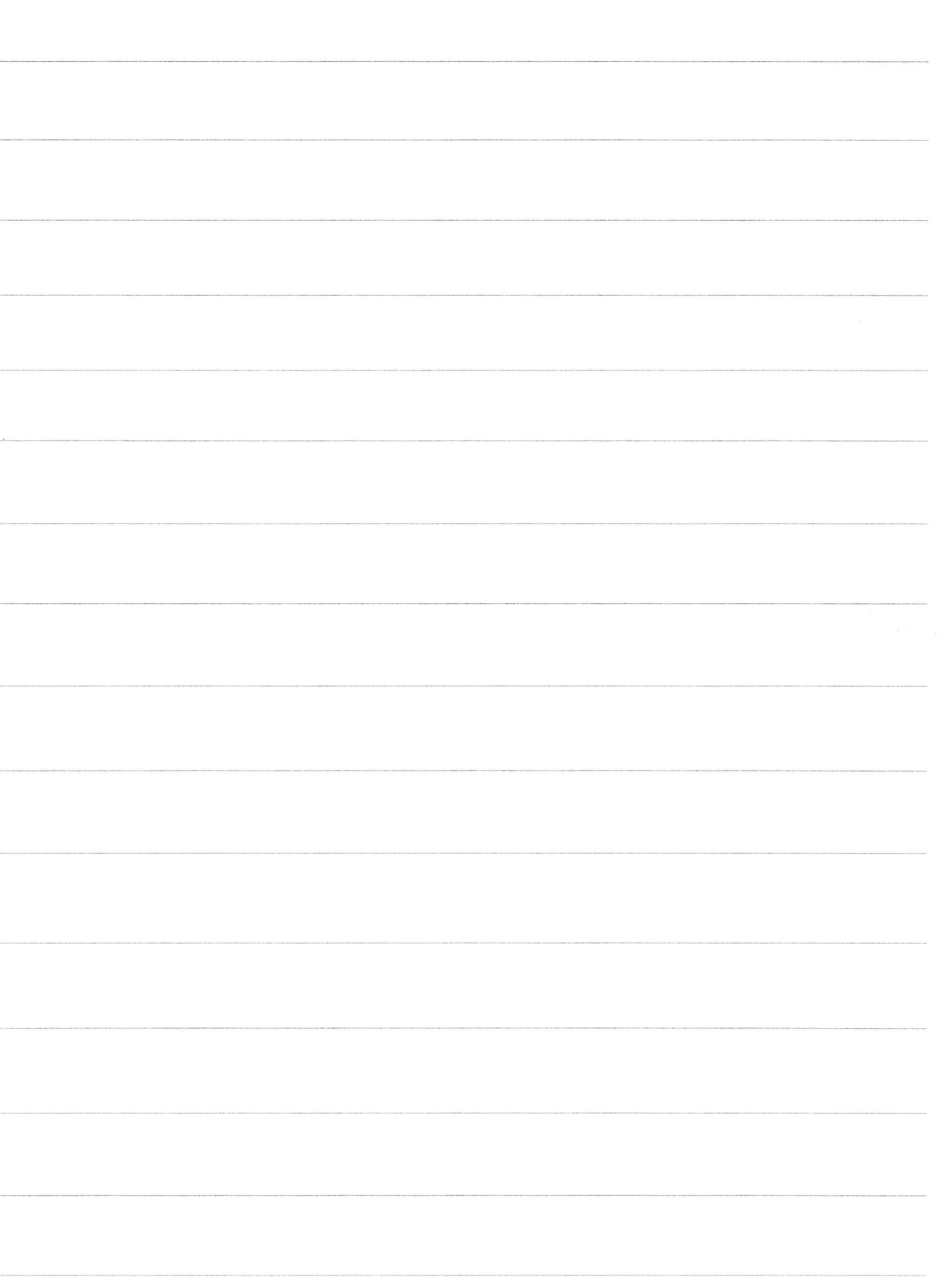

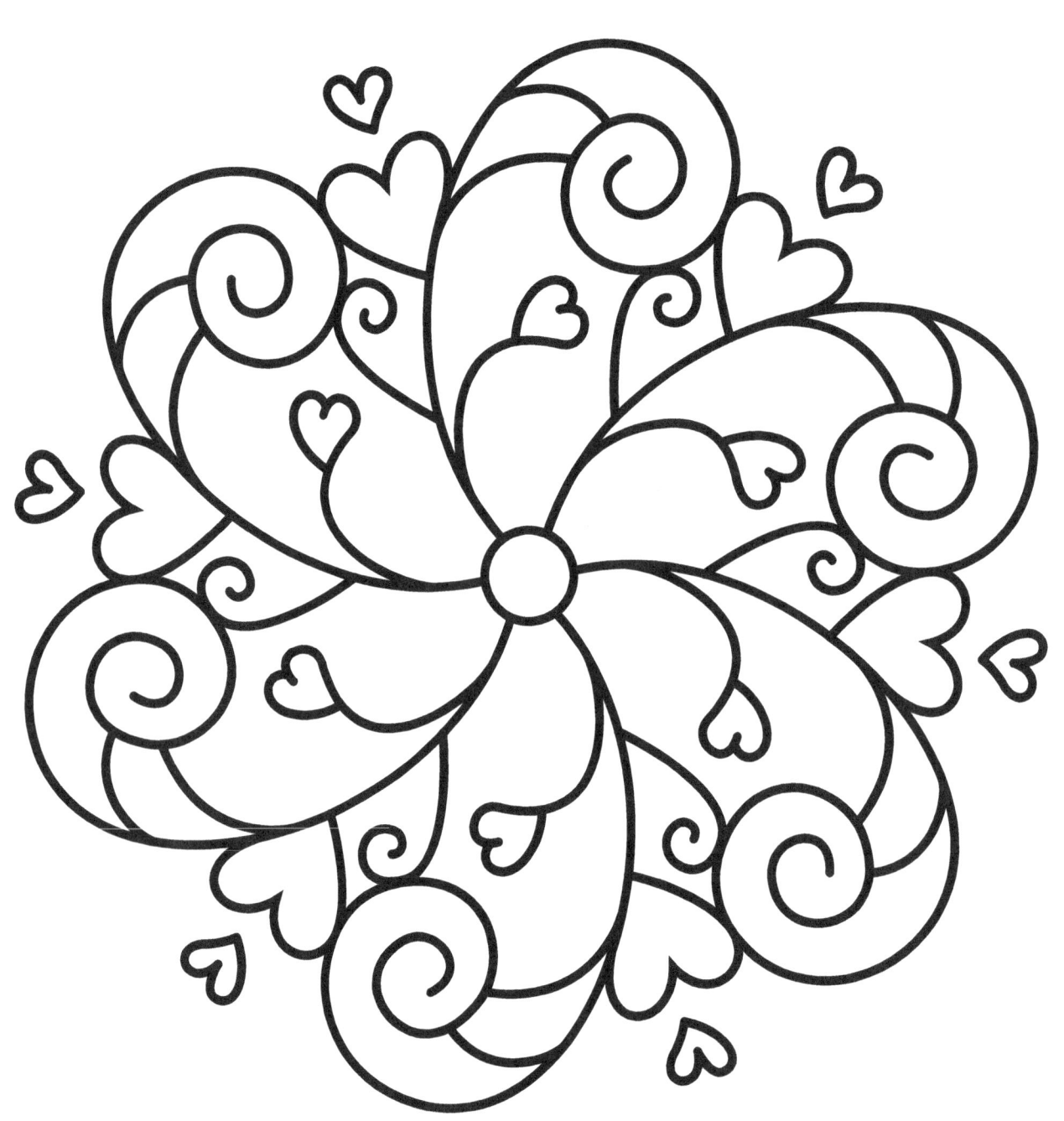

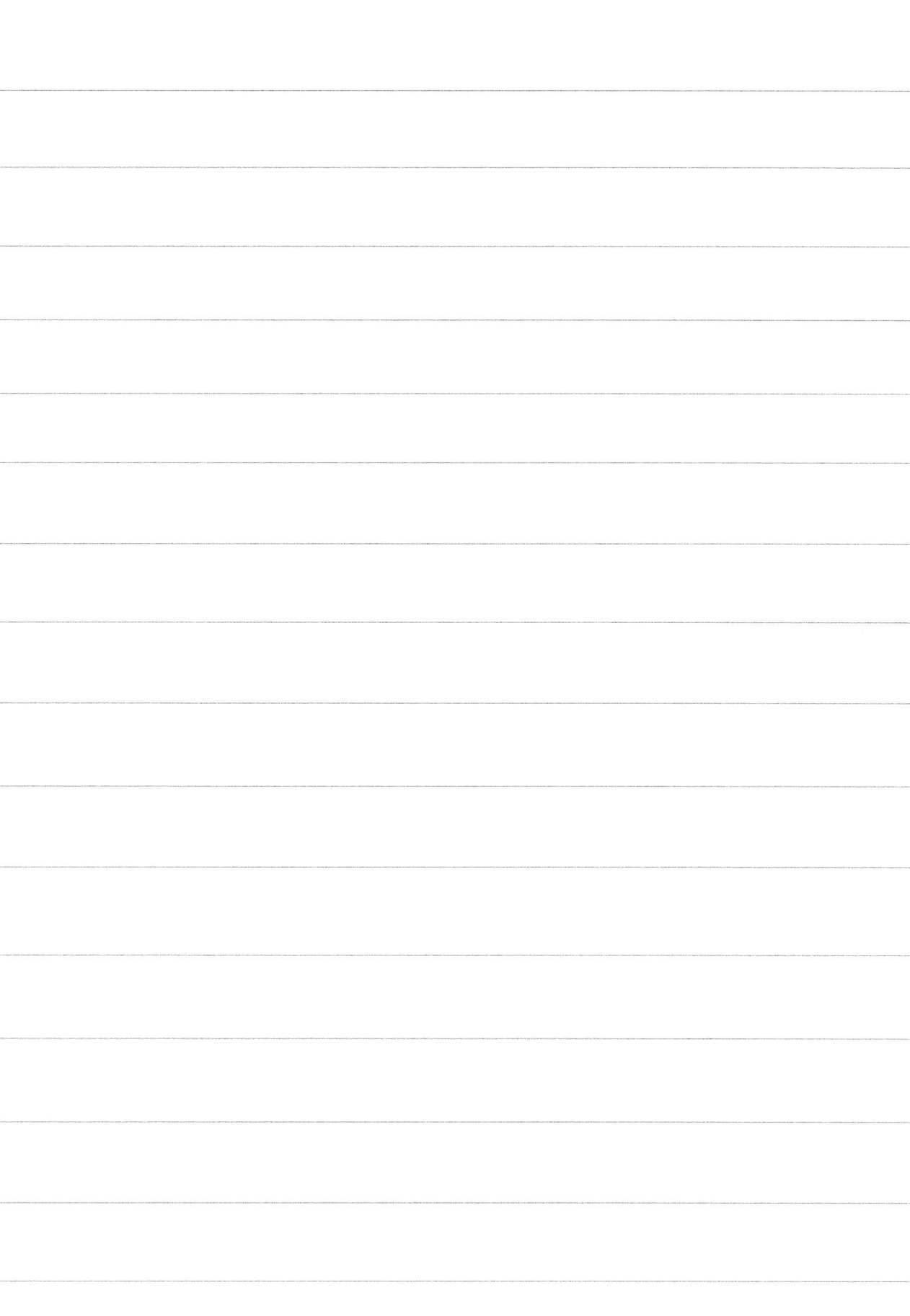

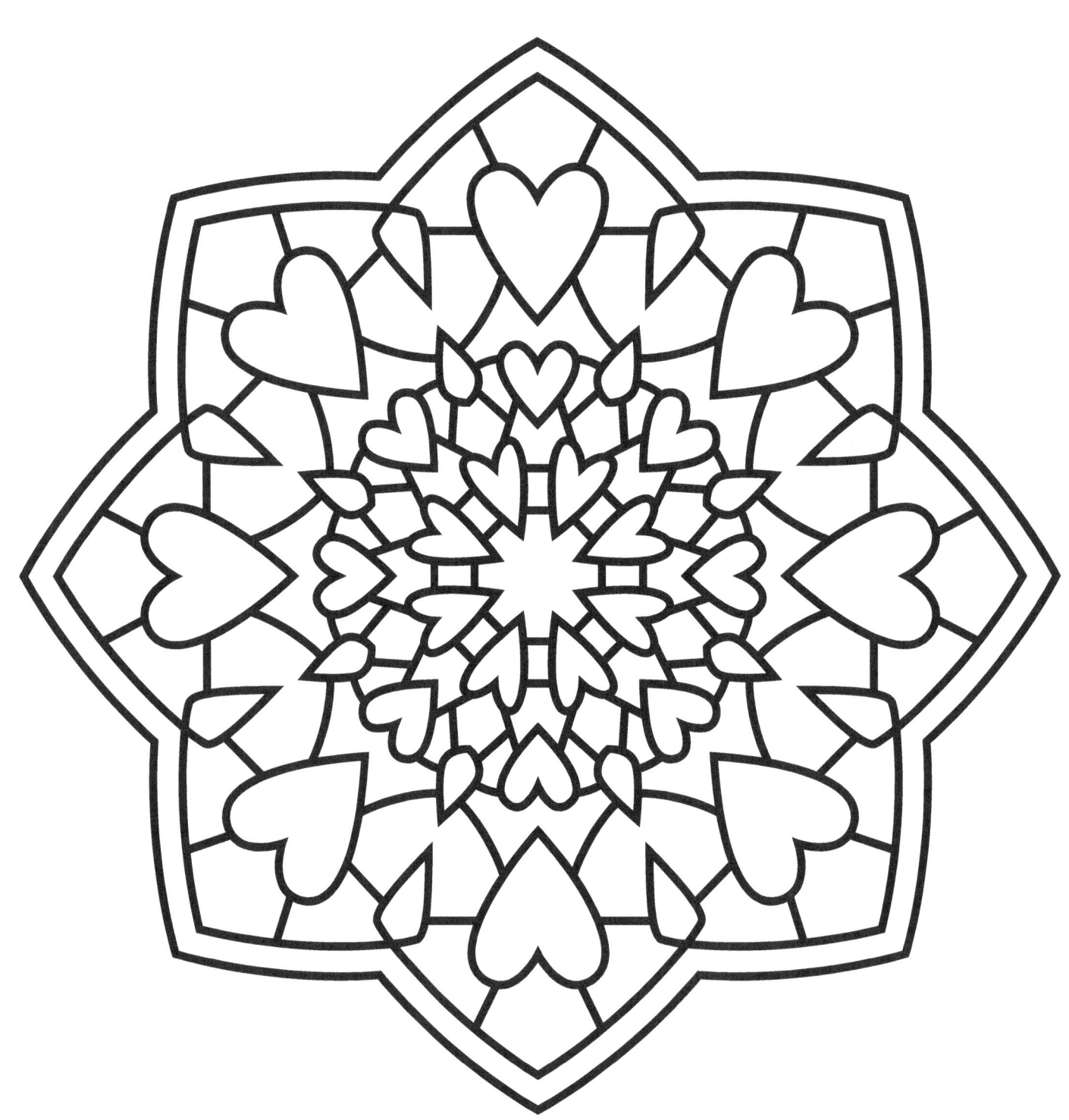

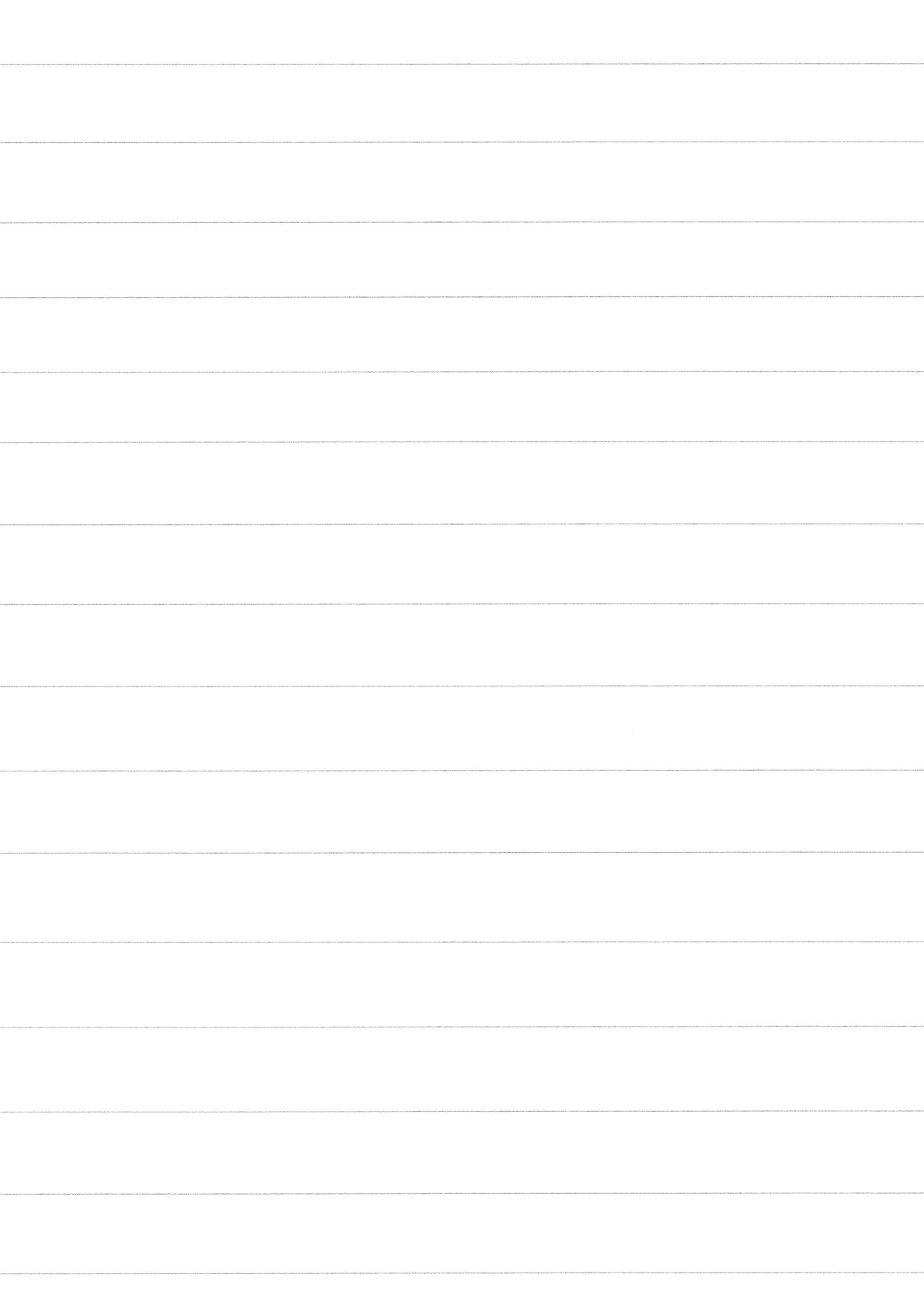

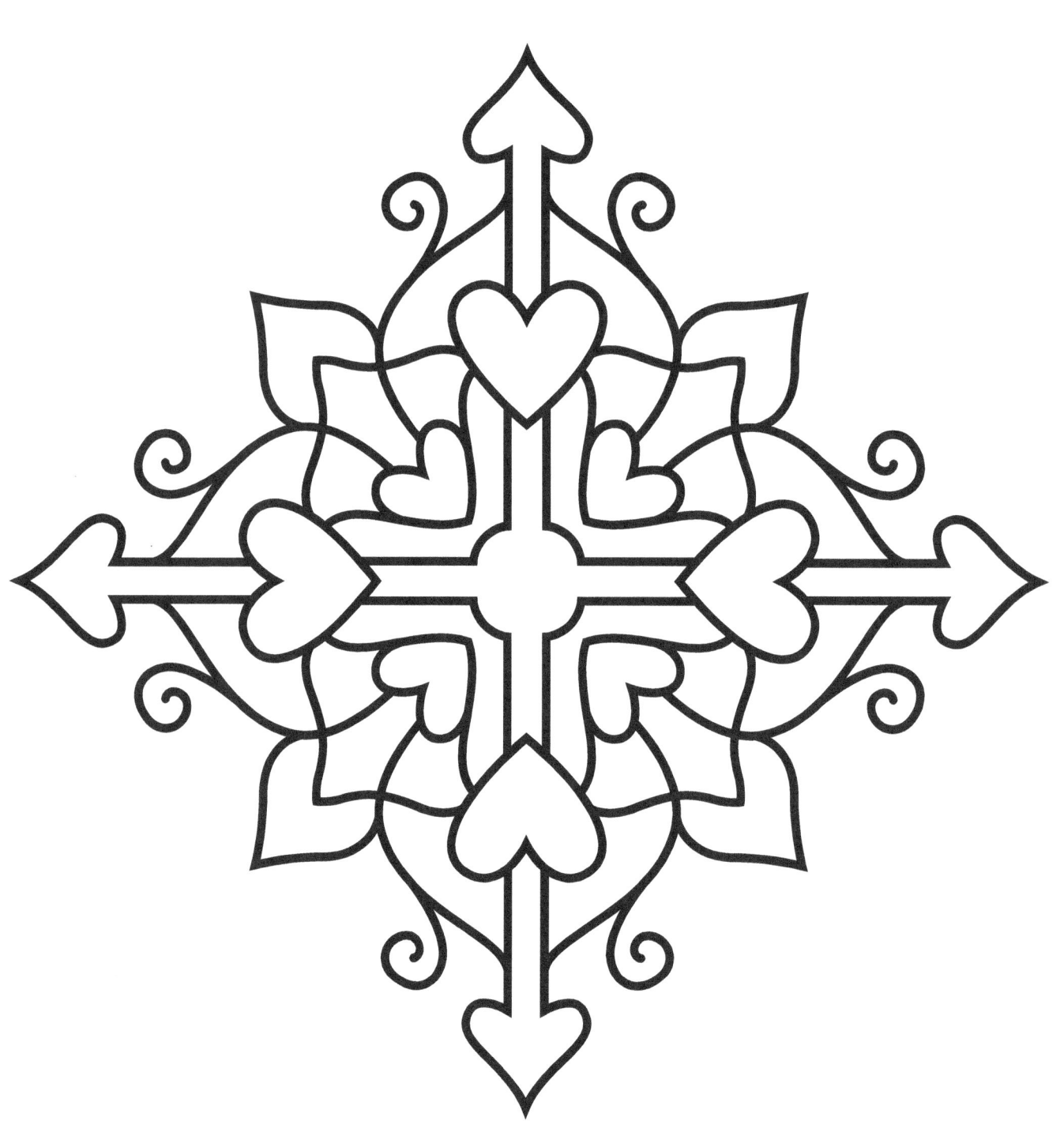

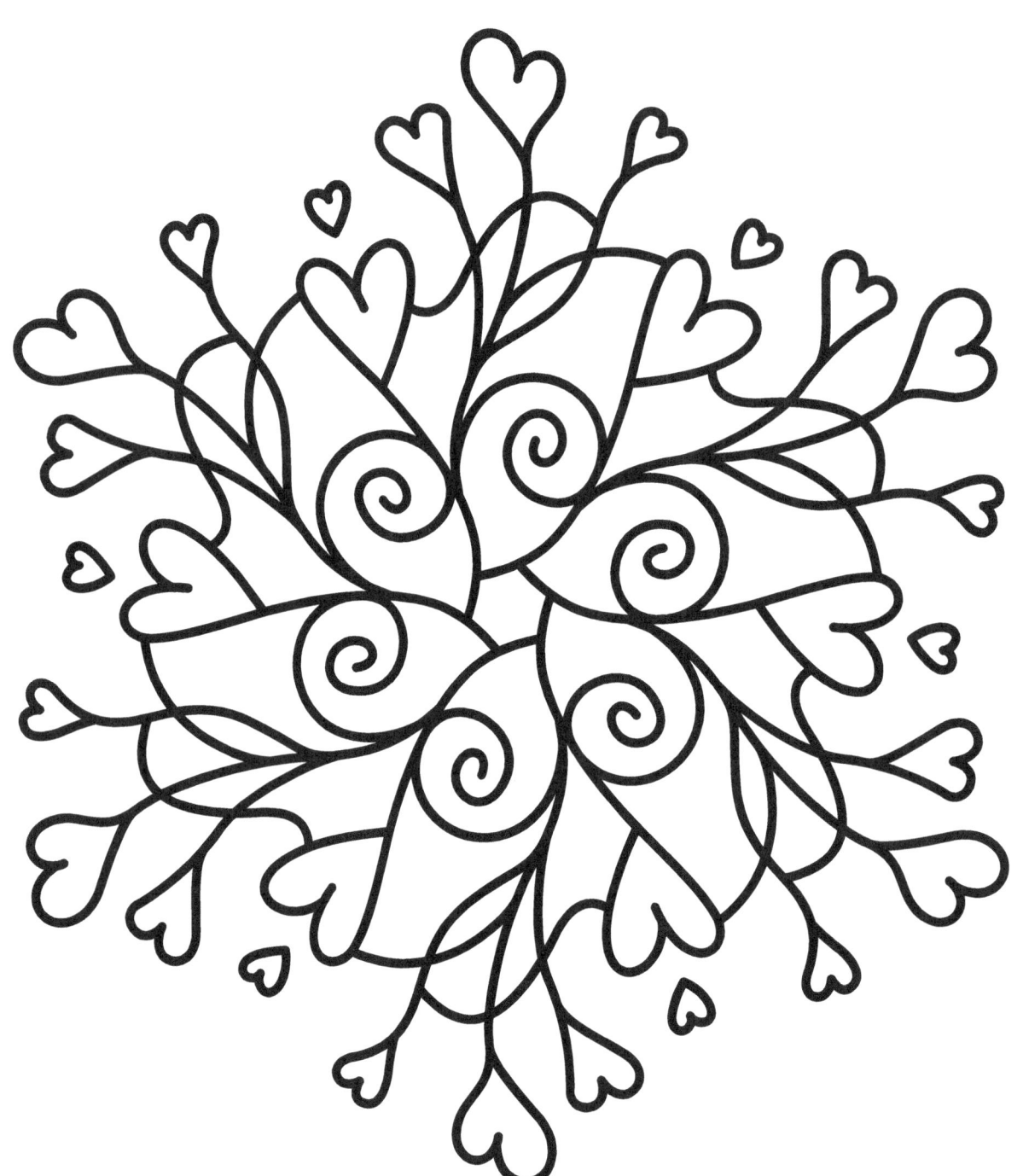

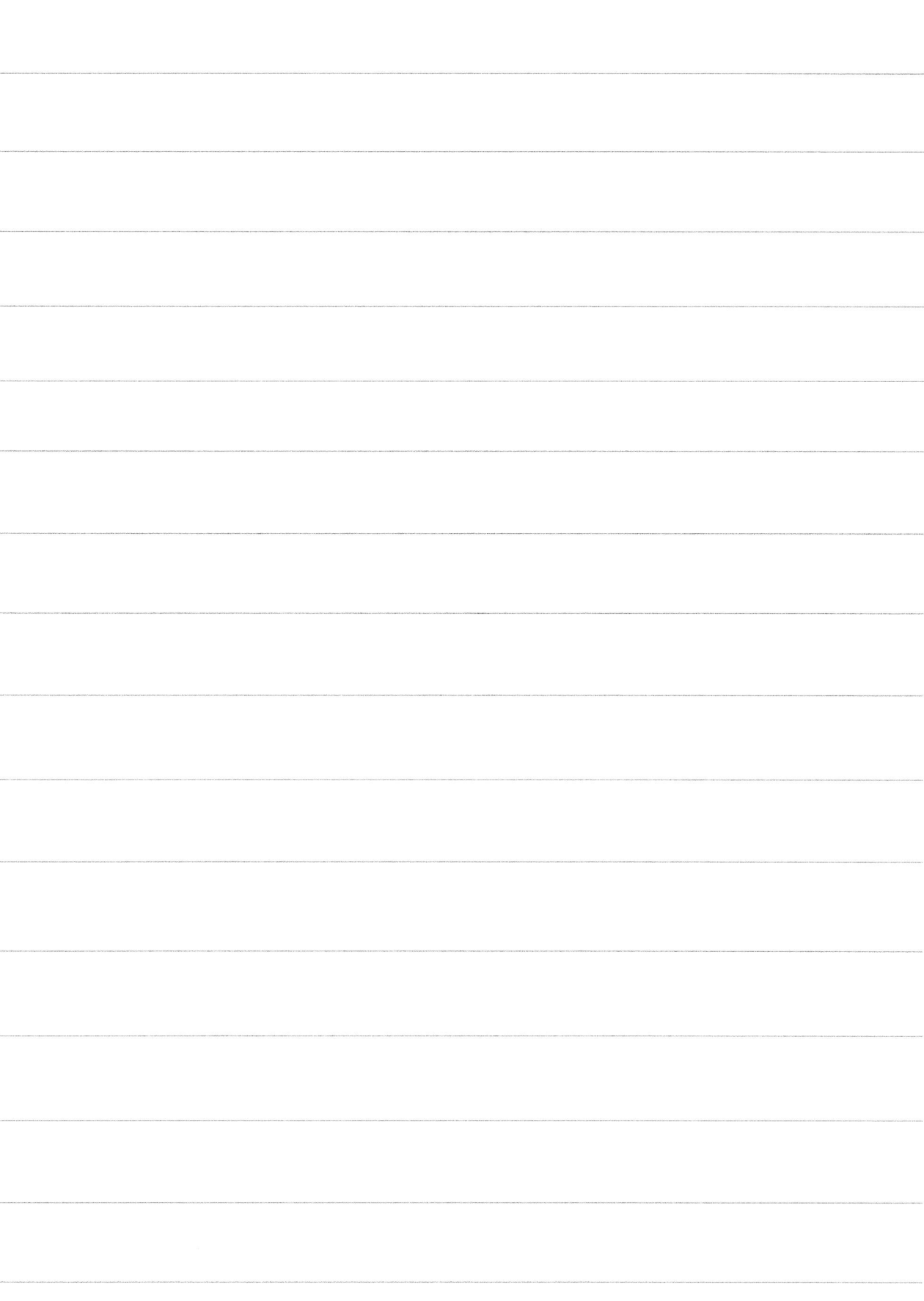

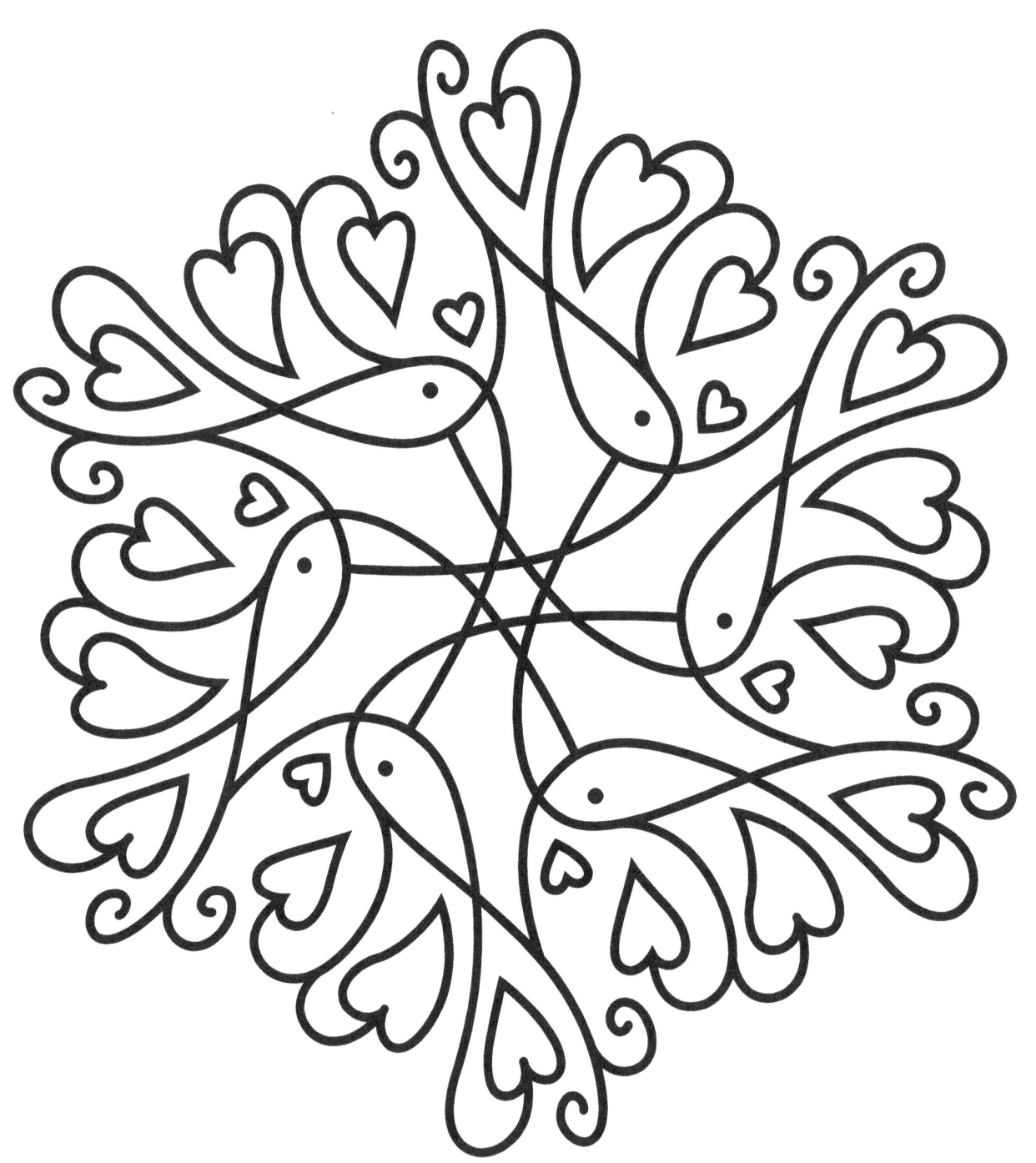

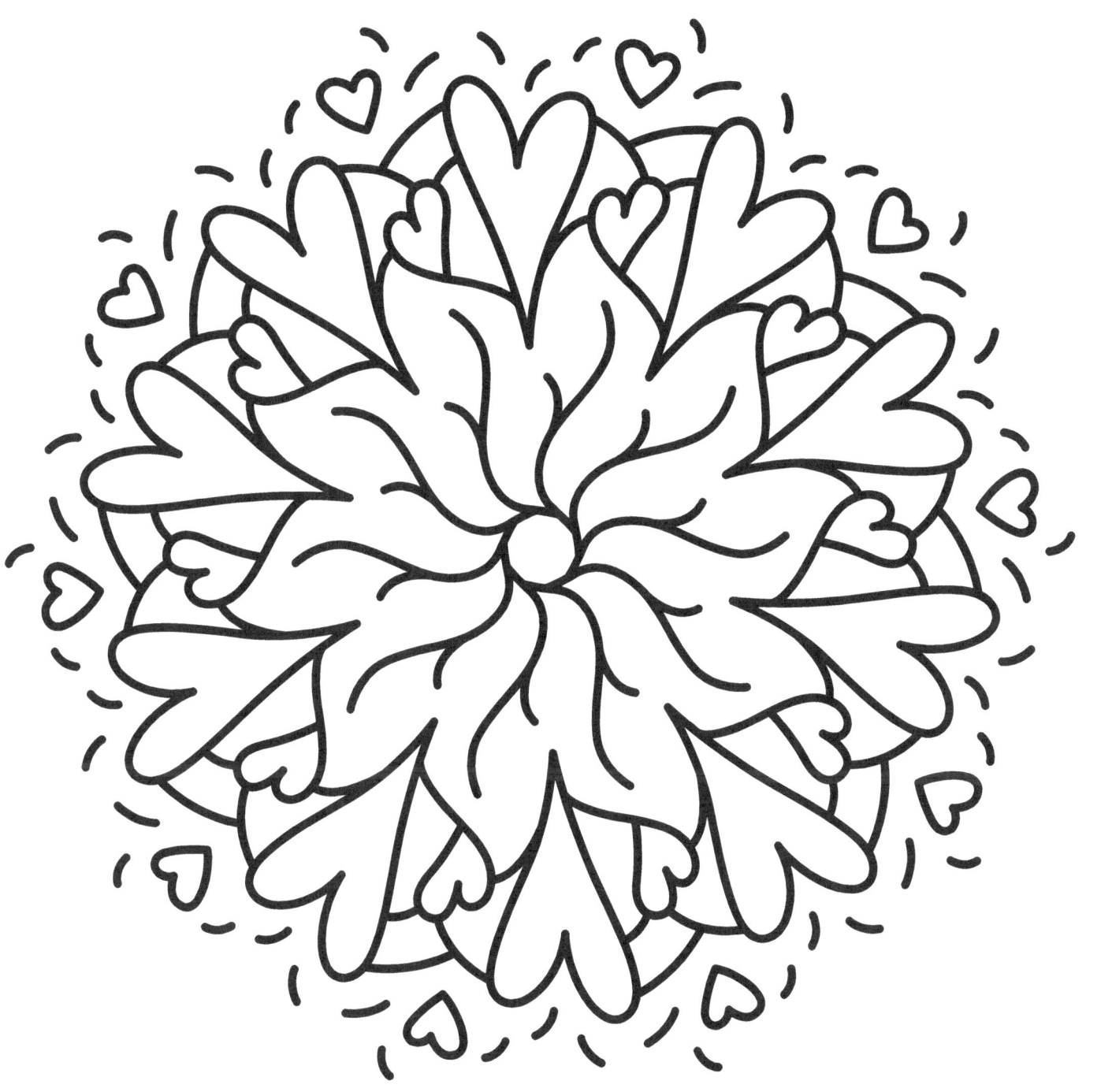

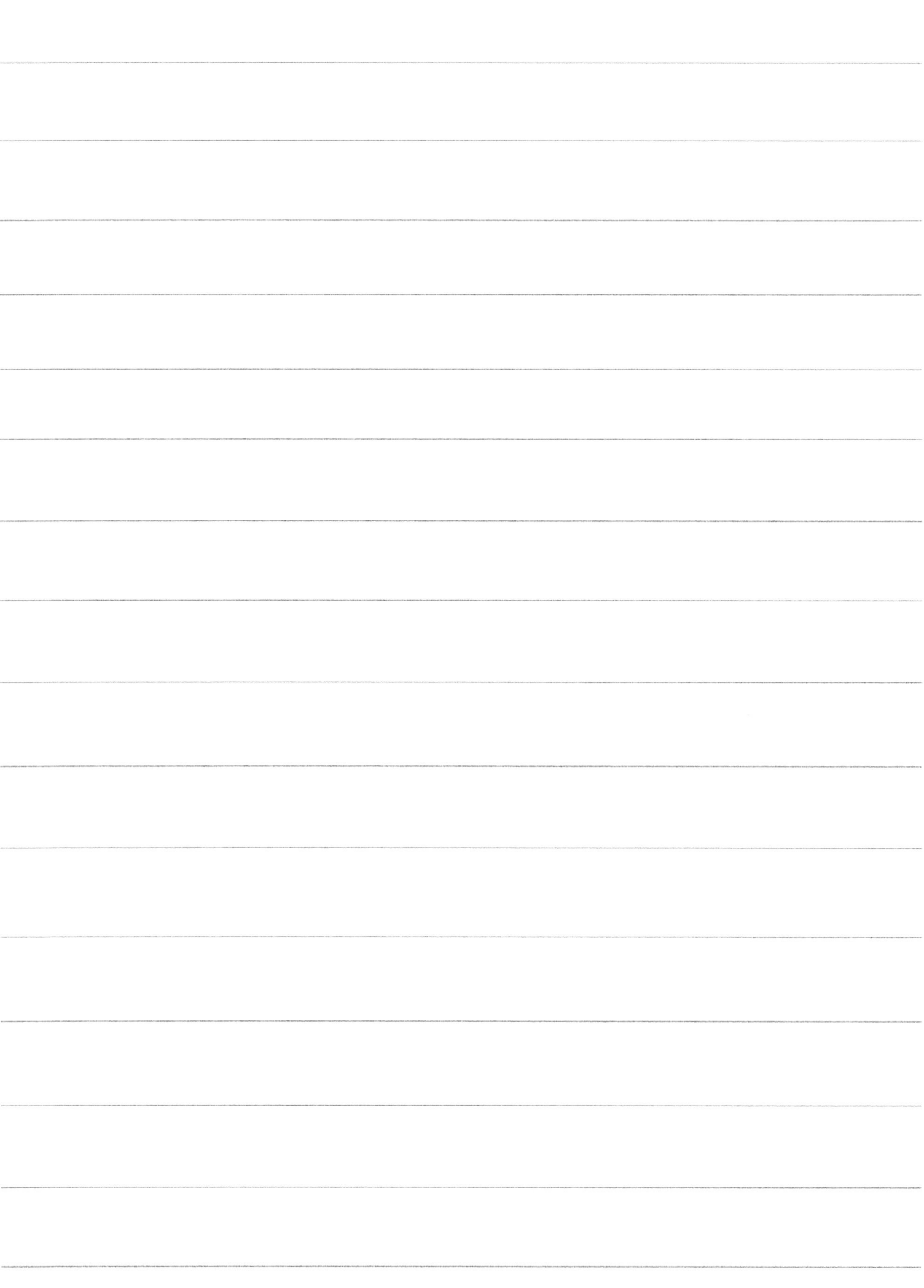

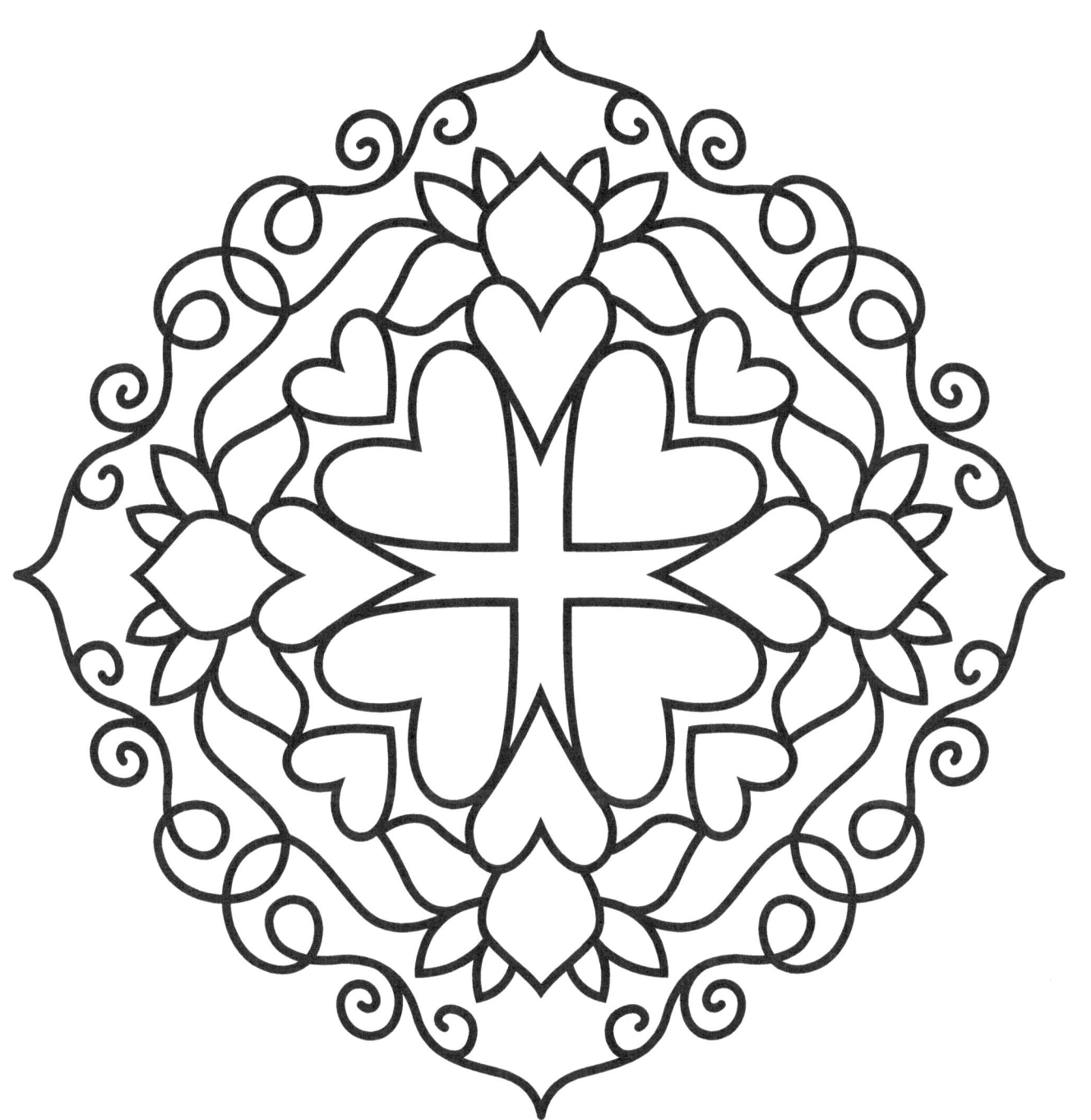

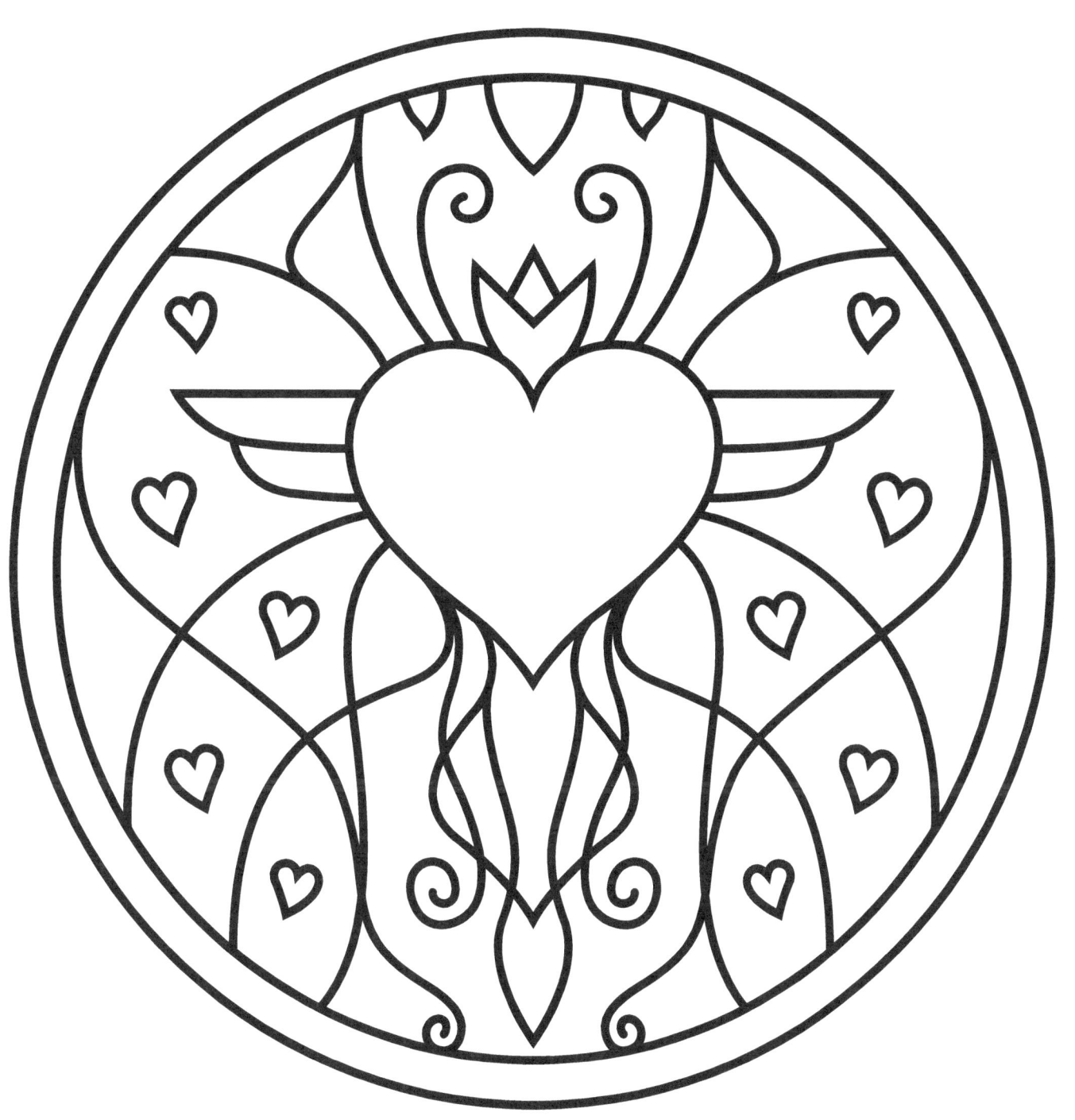

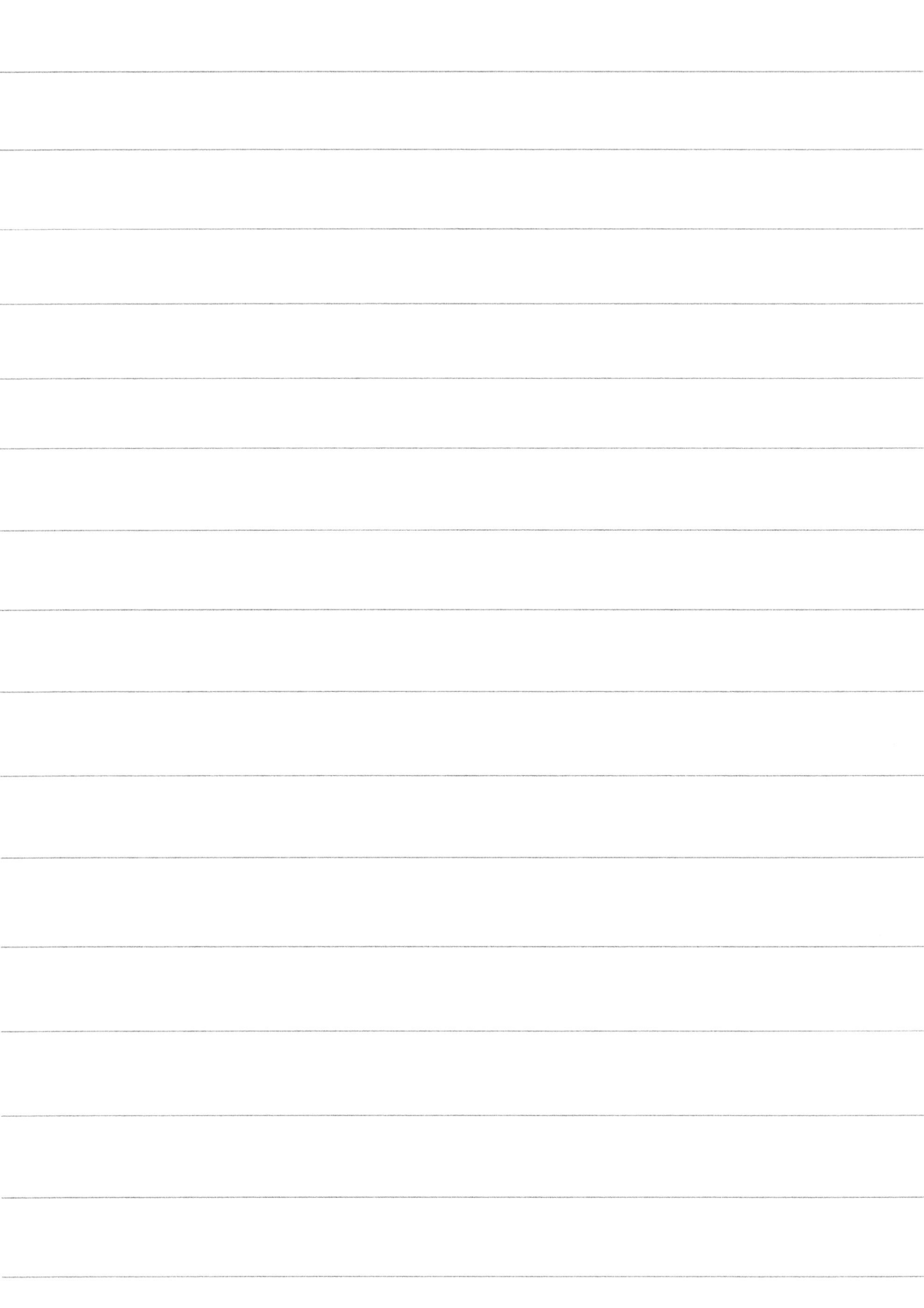

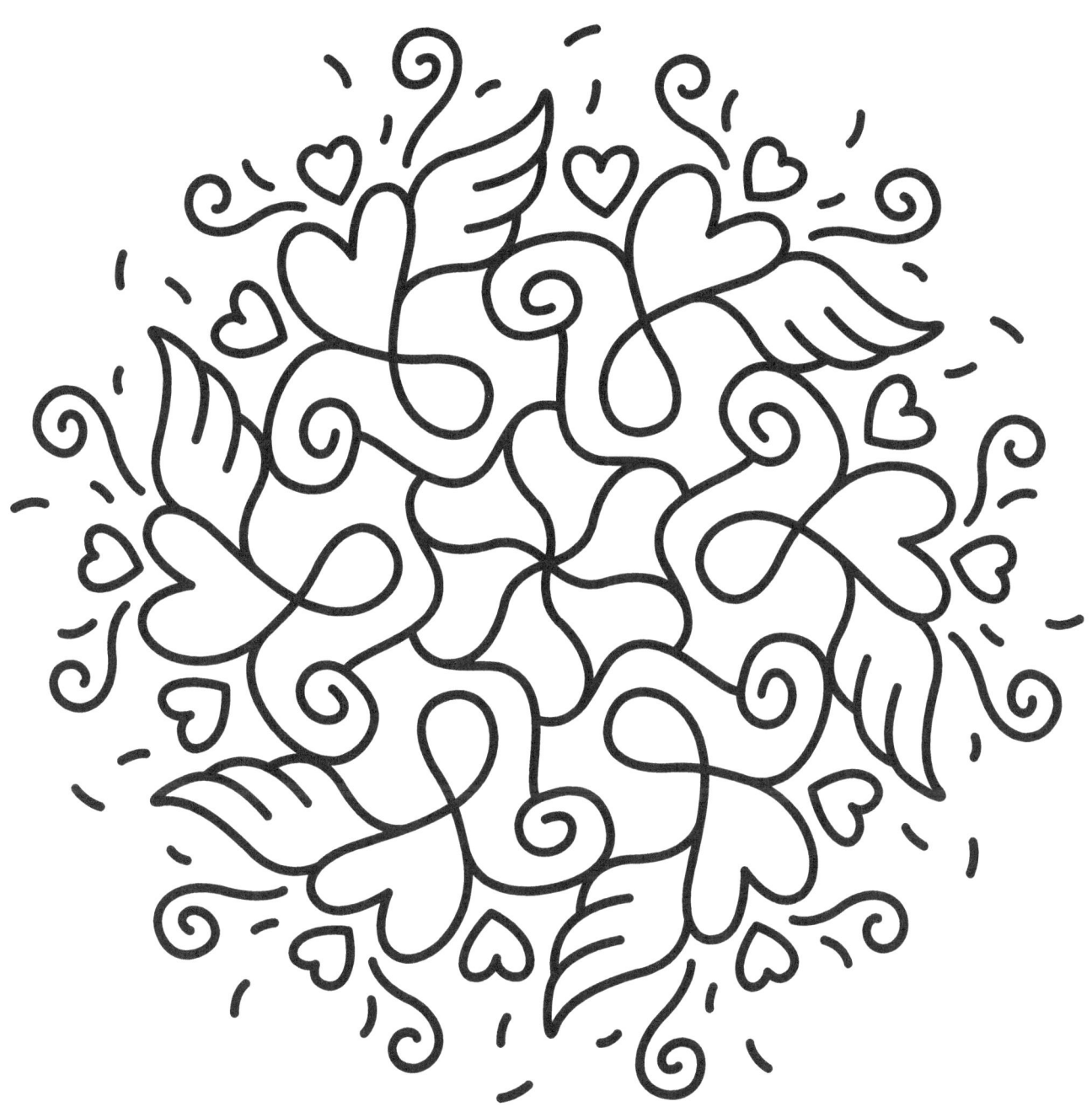

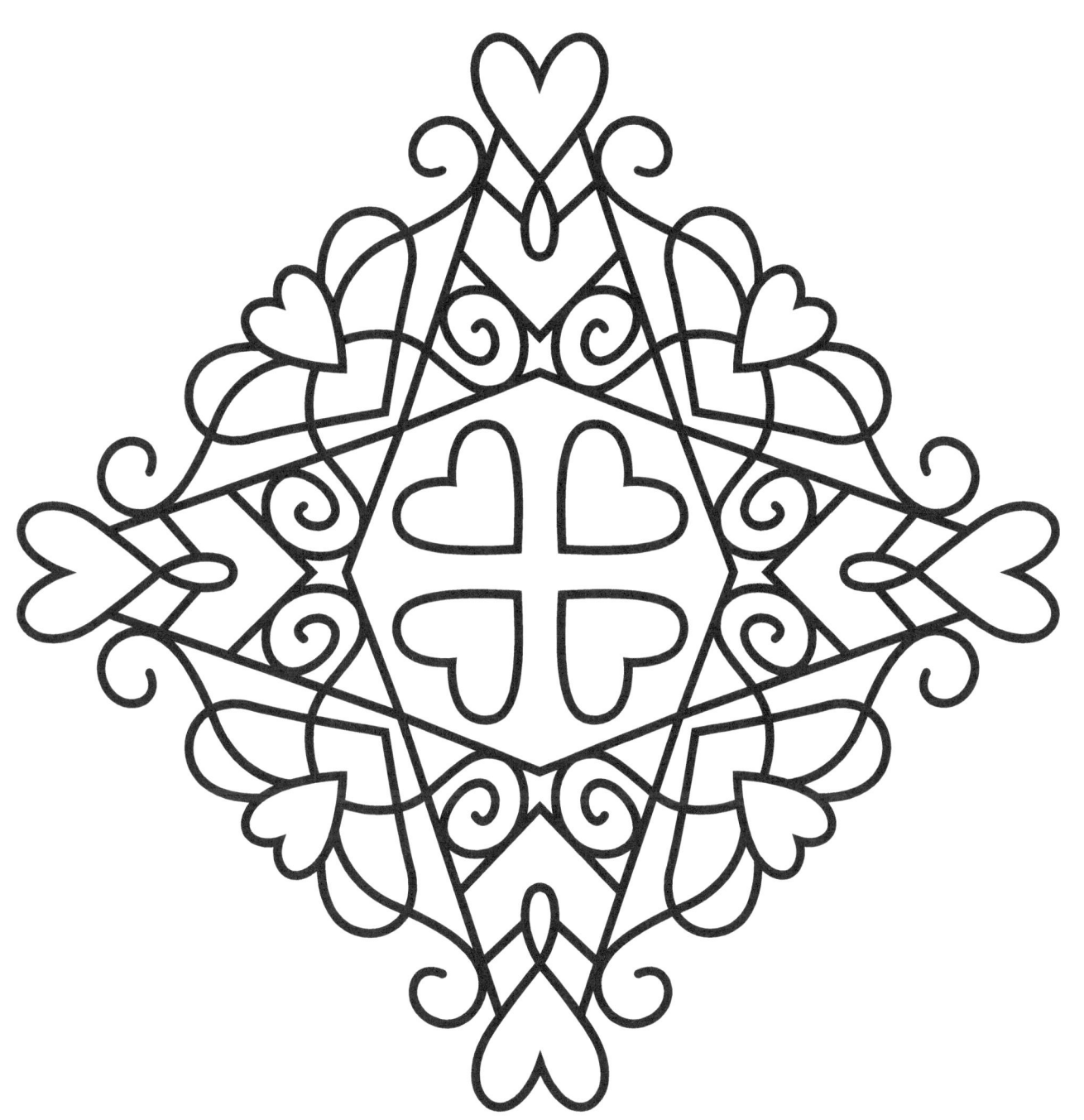

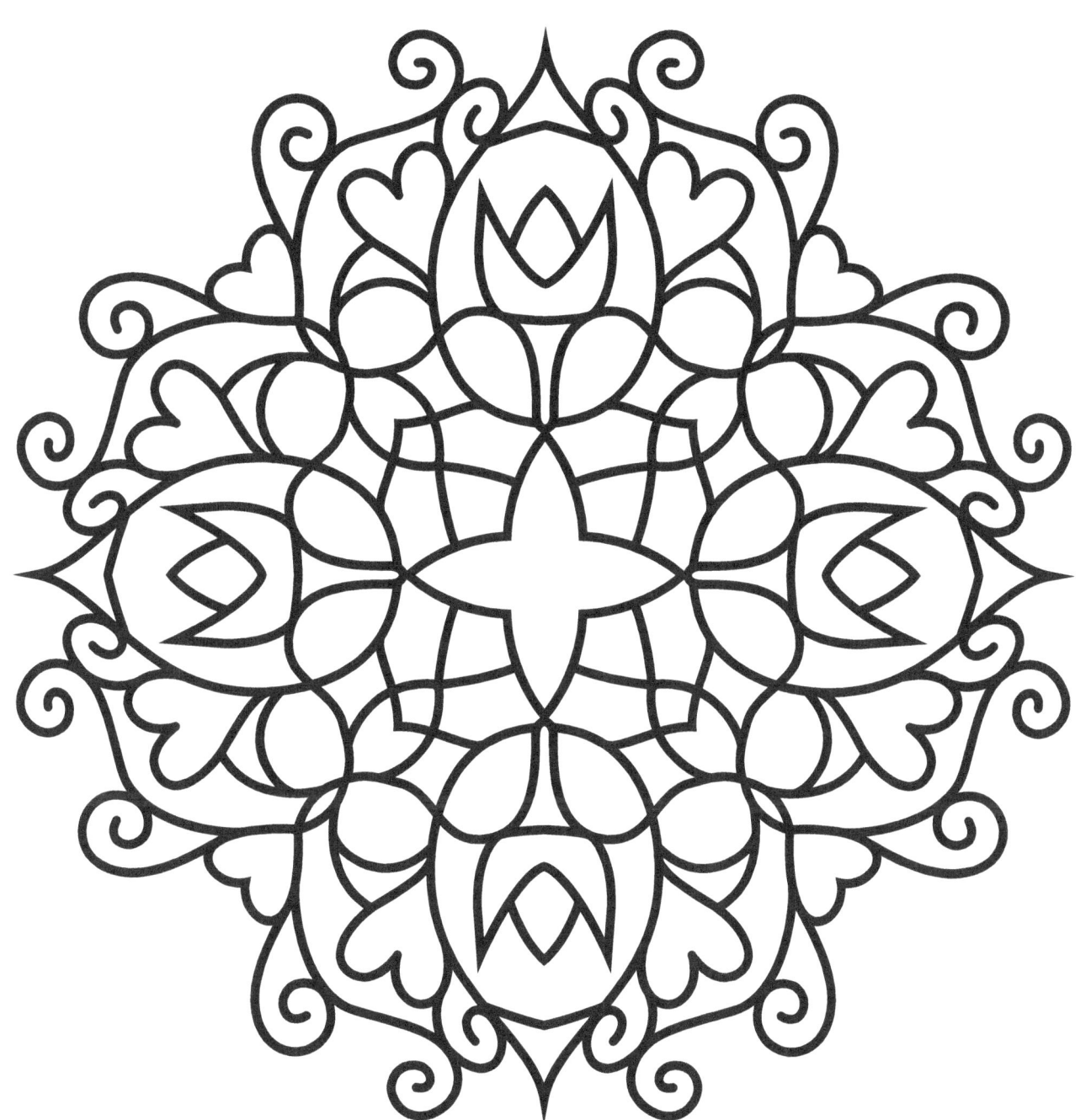

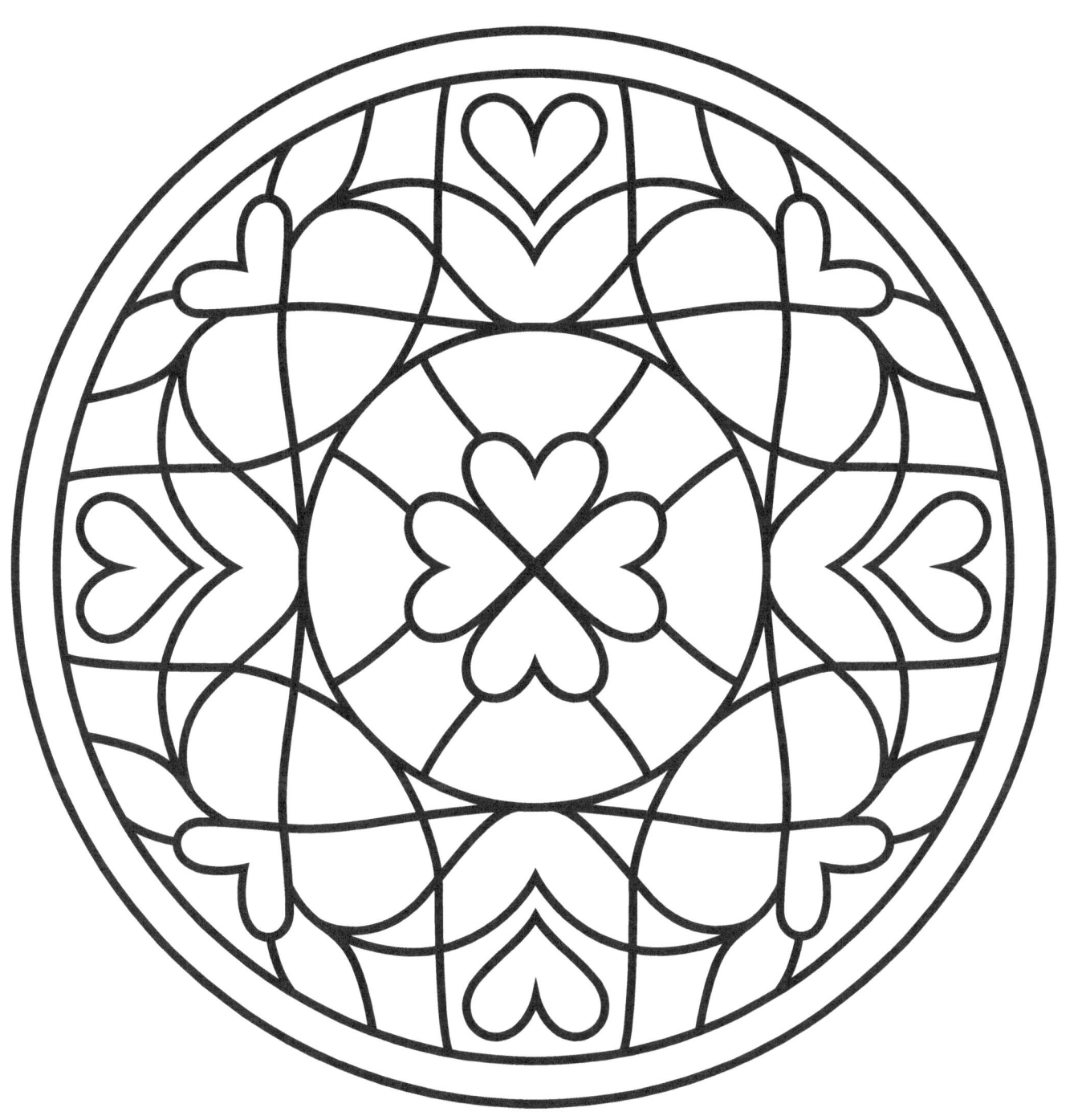

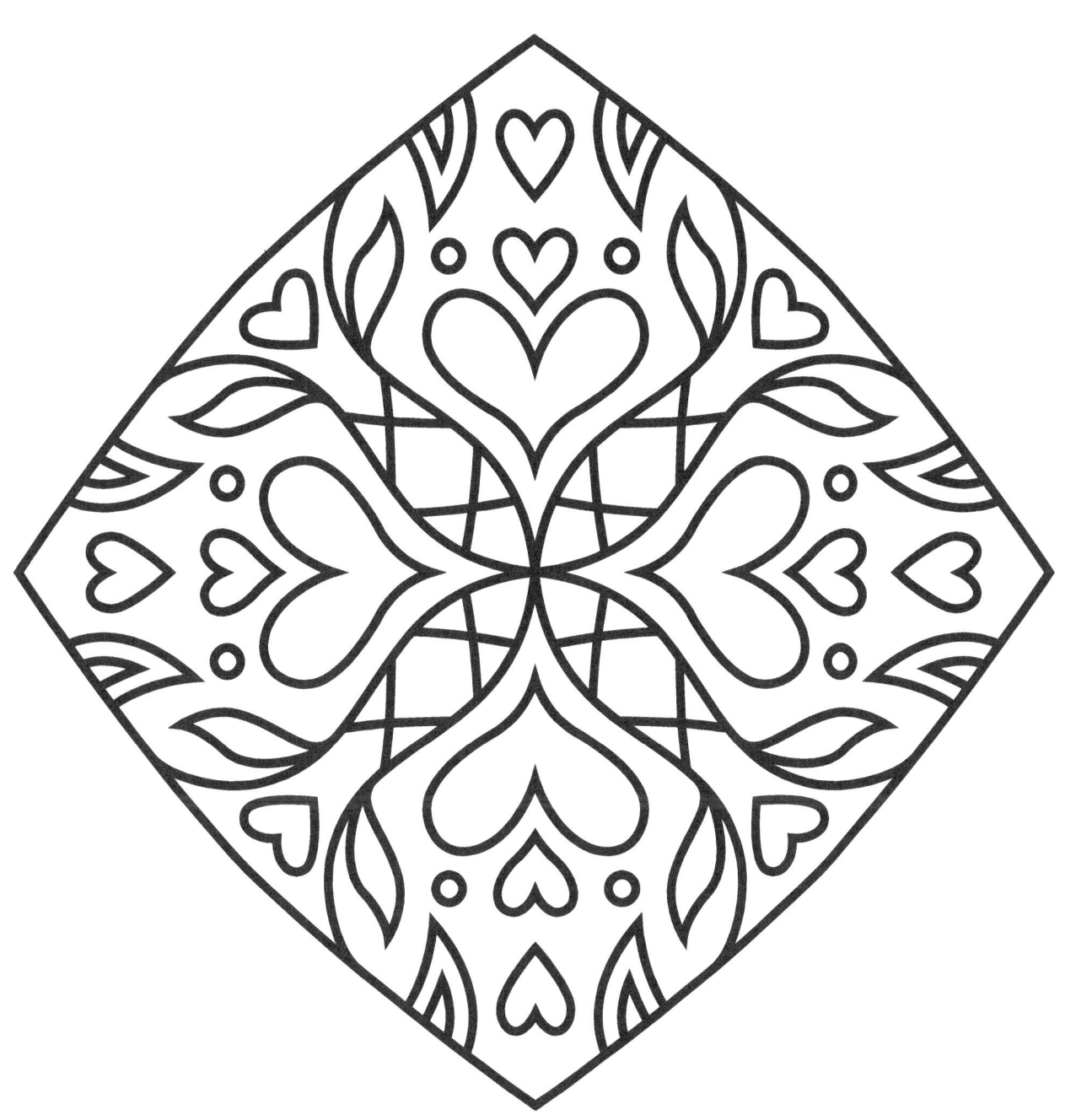

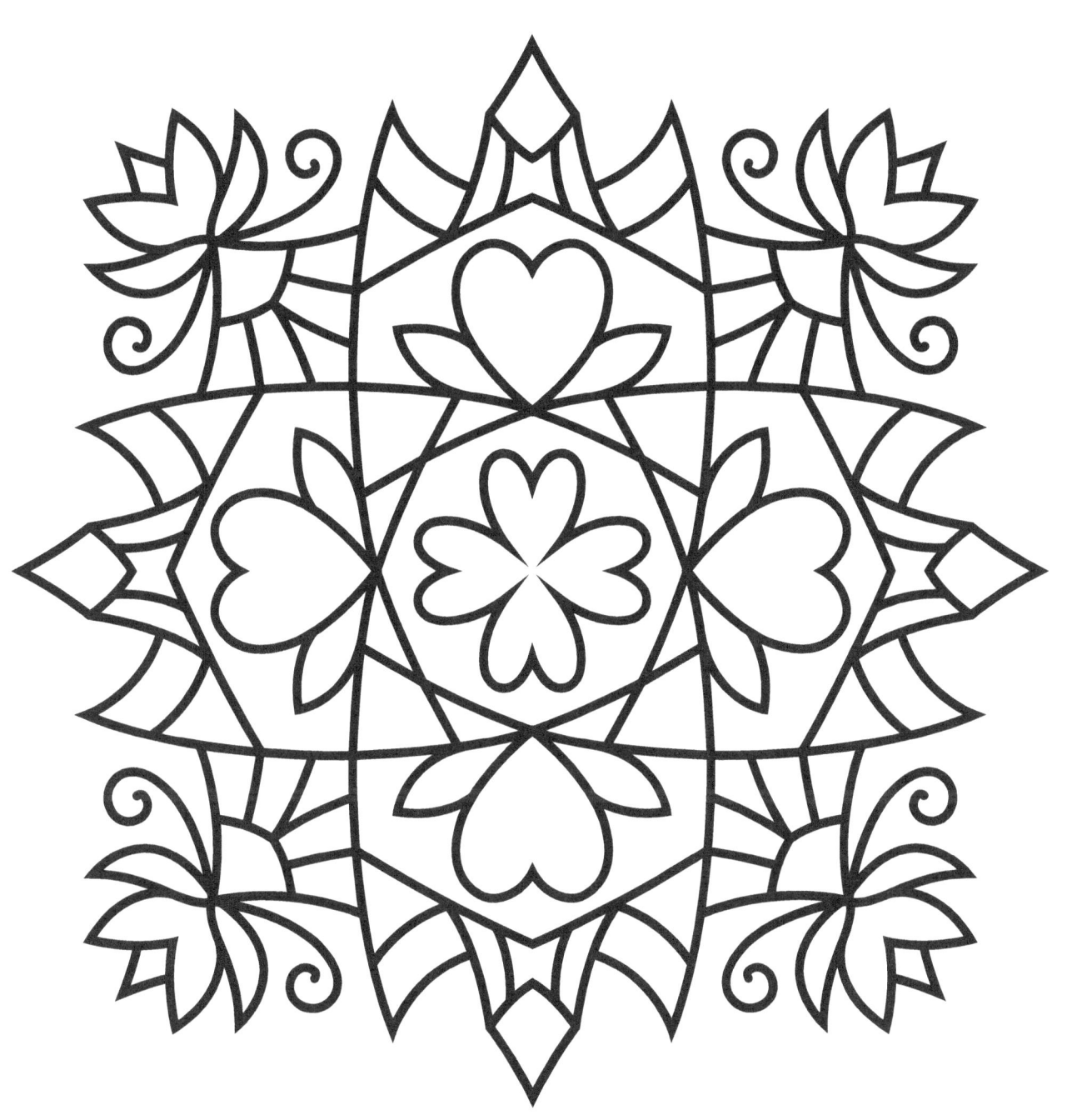

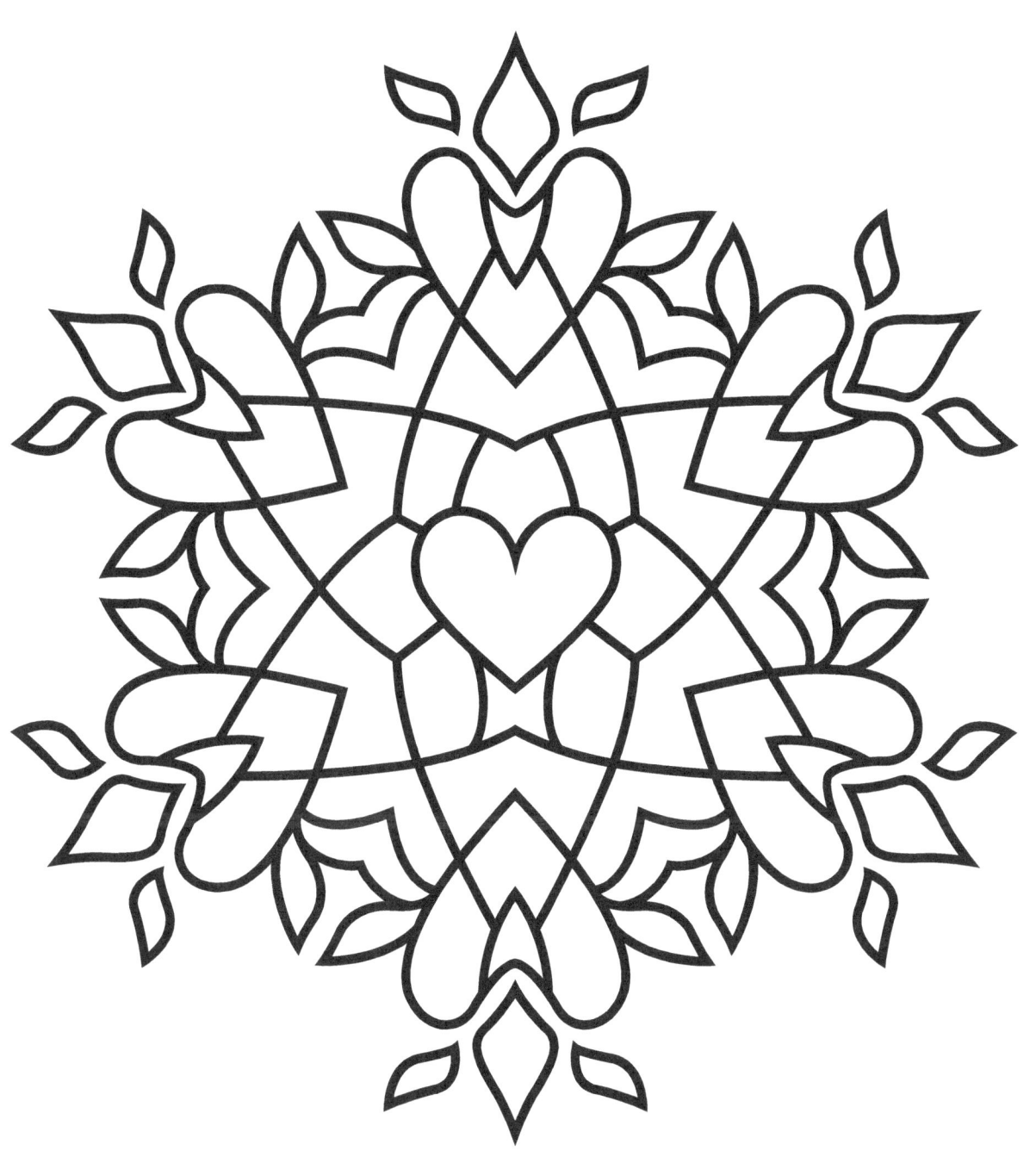

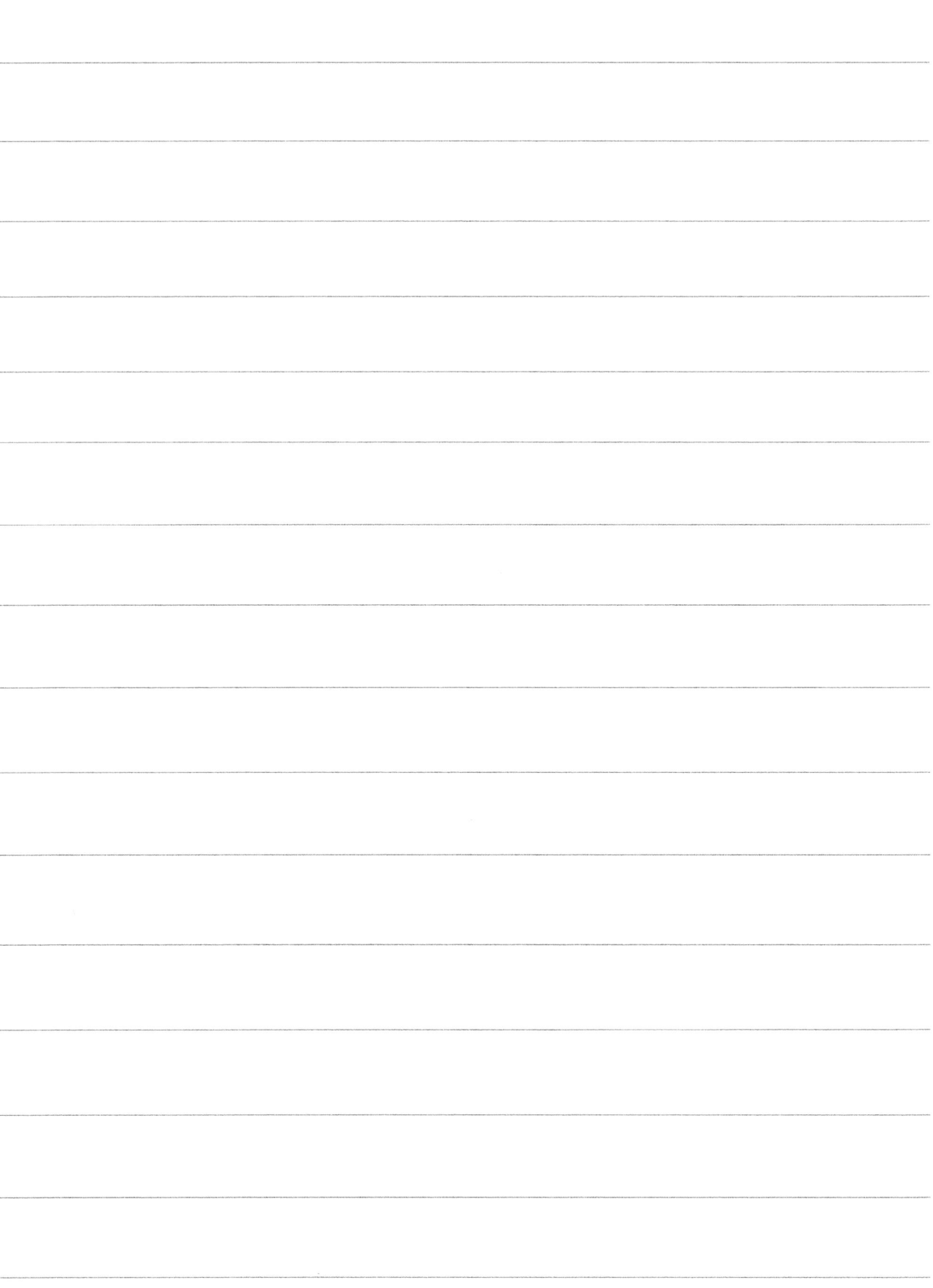

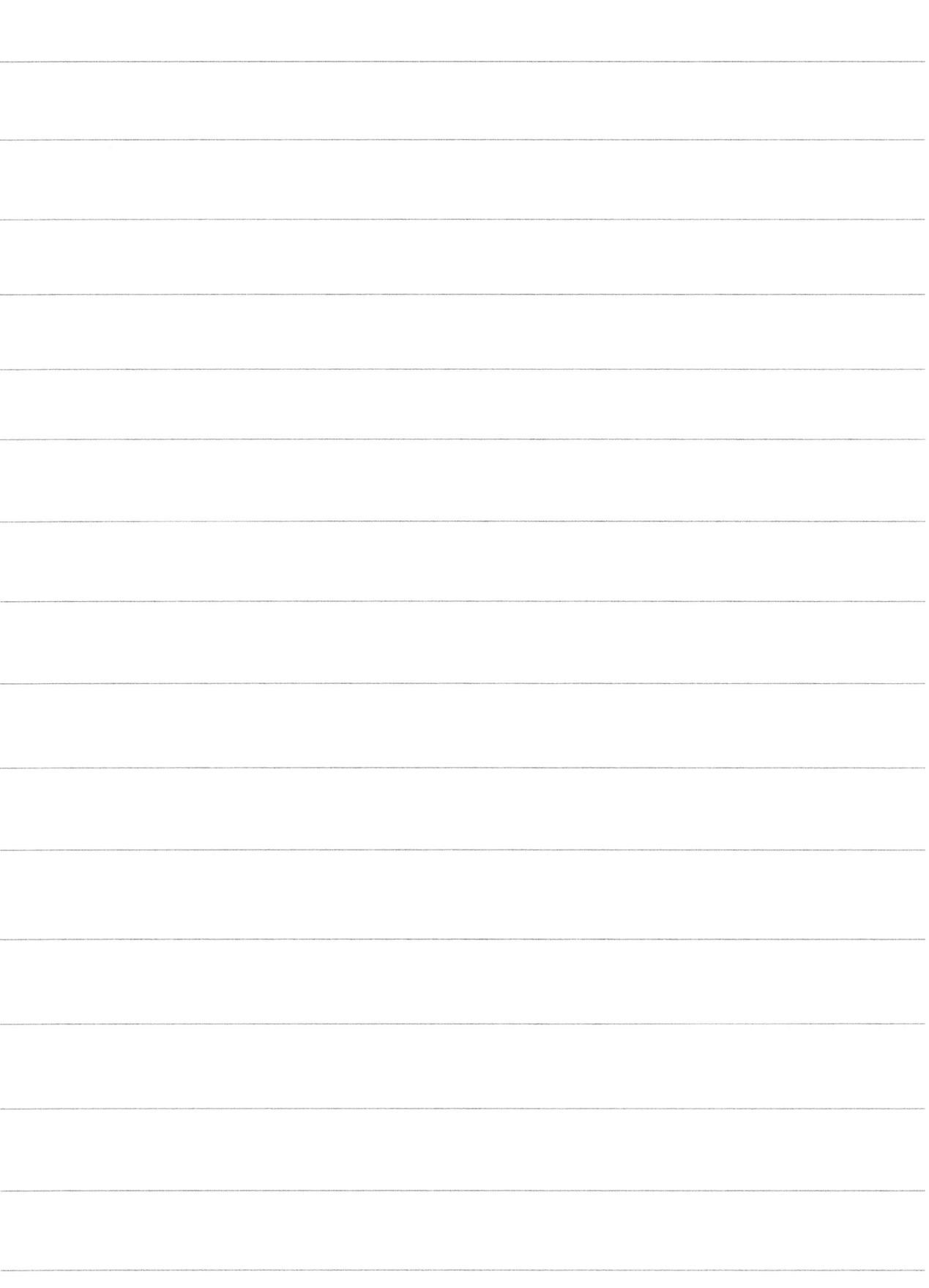

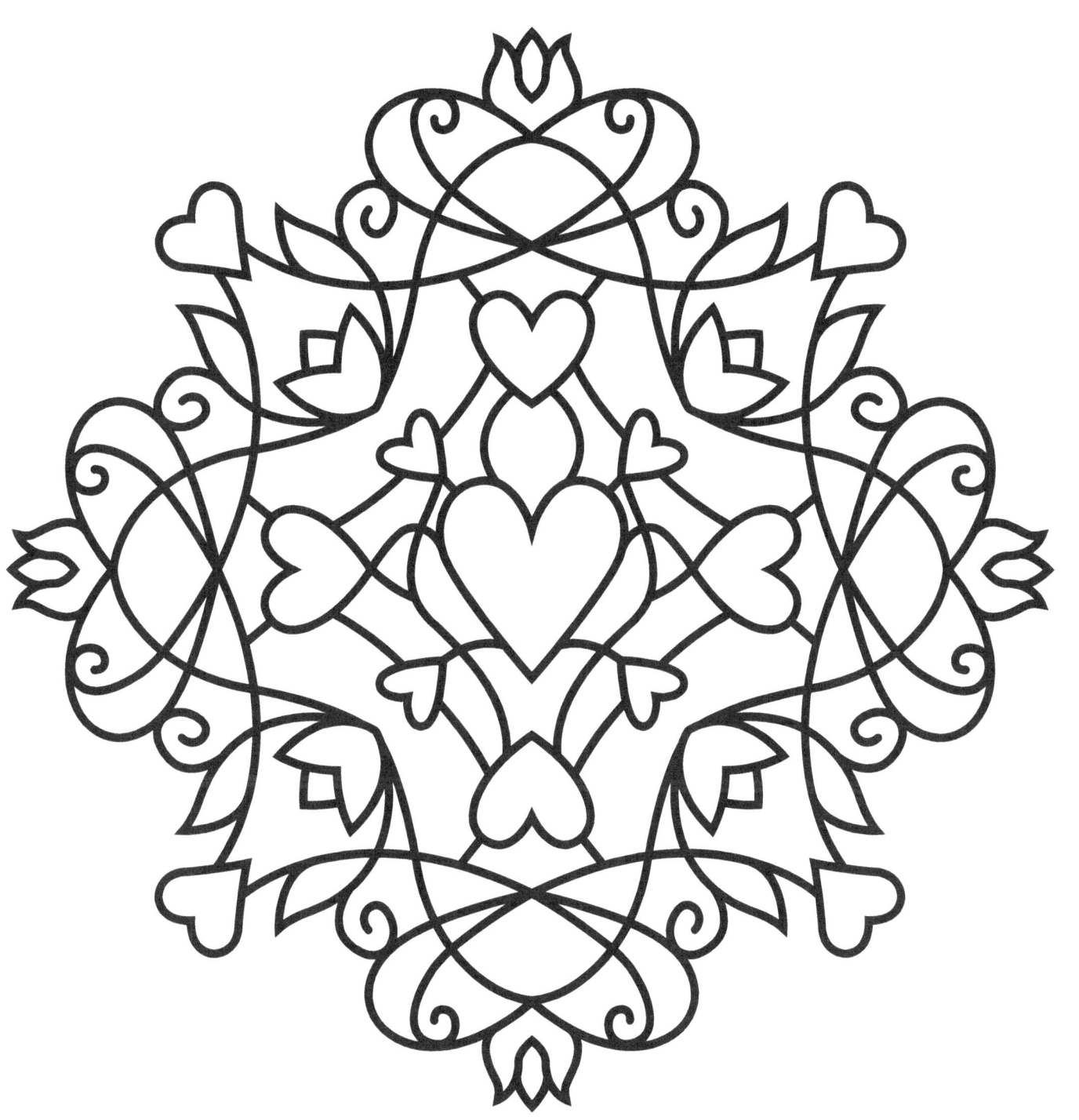

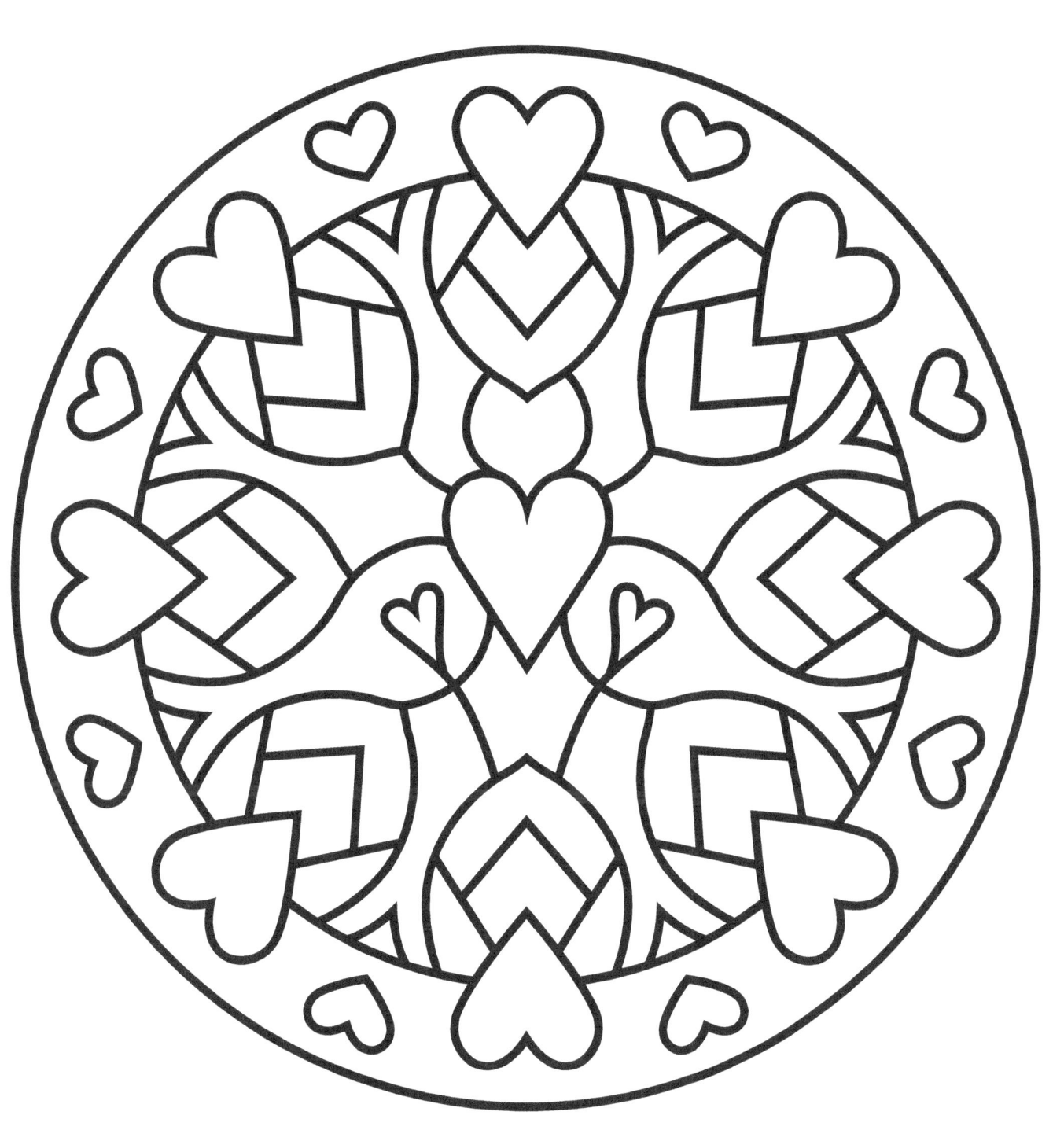